MW01051121

From Heartbreak to the Hippie Trail

Sex, Drugs, and Backpacking in Europe, Israel, East Africa, and Asia

Kenneth Liss

DEDICATION

For all those who claim "I never want to grow up," get out there and see the world. Seek out the unknown. Never let go of your sense of wonder. Then you'll stay young.

CONTENTS

LEAVING HOME

I think back to what precipitated my travel lust. It mainly had to do with losing my first wife, Suzy. To paraphrase one of my favorite comics, Bobcat Goldthwait, "Well, I didn't really lose her. I knew where she was. She was just doing it with someone else." The someone else was a good friend.

It was the early '70s, a time when a large group of couples and some singles used to party virtually every weekend, always finding a great venue for our mirth. We drank a lot and took copious amounts of drugs. Once Suzy left me, it became less and less enjoyable to be with my crowd since I'd always be running into Suzy and my ex-friend.

I decided I needed to get out of Dodge and bought a one-way ticket for a charter flight to London. I still had a month and a half to go after purchasing the ticket, but just knowing I was getting out of town gave me a good feeling and allowed me time to tie up loose ends.

I was a warehouseman at the time and was on the phone one day with Donna, my contact at 3M company in Los Angeles. We bought a lot of indoor and outdoor carpeting from them. "Donna, this might be the last of my monthly calls to order your products. I'm going to quit my job and go travel, starting off in London. The main reason I'm leaving's because my wife and I have split up and I'm pretty free now to do something new."

Donna responded with some irony. "That's interesting, Ken, because my husband and I just separated too. Our divorce is in the works. Hey, d'you ever come to Los Angeles for any reason? If you're down here, you should look me up."

"Well, my friend, I really don't ever come down but, if this is an invitation, I'll come. How's this weekend?"

"Sounds terrific, Ken! We could go camping out at some great campground on the Kern River, several hours east of where I live in Southern California."

"OK, I'll see you this Friday and meet you at Orange County airport."

"I have a yellow Volkswagen bug. Let me know what time your flight arrives and I'll pull up and get you."

1

Friday arrived and I flew down there. I was standing in the terminal and could see cars as they pulled up. Soon I spotted a yellow bug and getting out of it was a large — very large — woman who wasn't the least bit attractive. I told myself if she came up to me and asked if I was Ken, I'd tell her no. Luckily, she didn't approach me, but she did pick up an older gentleman.

Ten minutes later, another yellow bug pulled up and this time a very attractive girl got out. Medium height, slim, and with a head of curly brown hair, she came over to me, said my name, and we hugged, walked back to her car, and drove back to her house. She had some snacks and beer for me and afterwards we started fooling around but she stopped me short of going all the way.

"Ken, let's wait for tomorrow if you don't mind." That was a little disappointing but what the hay. No problem. She showed me where to sleep and told me, "I've an early morning appointment tomorrow and I'll be back by 10 a.m. Help yourself to anything in the fridge and, when I'm back, we'll pack the car and leave for Kern River."

The next morning, after she'd returned from her appointment, we put all her gear in the car and headed east. During the first hour, all seemed to be fine. There was plenty of conversation about everything imaginable, but mostly the breakups we'd both experienced, and a little about my upcoming trip. Then around the two-hour mark after we left, it got pretty quiet in the car. Conversation all of a sudden became strained.

After twenty minutes of relative silence, Donna turned to me and said, "Maybe we should go back to L.A." She then turned the car around and started heading back.

I was startled. "Donna, I came all the way from San Francisco for this! How about you reconsider and we go camping?"

She thought about it and turned around again, heading toward our Kern River destination. We made it there by late afternoon. What a gorgeous place the Kern River was, just perfect for a romantic weekend with a new lady in my life. We had a cooler full of beer, cold cuts, bread, and some snacks and cookies. We found a great spot just a few yards from the river where we drank beer and, as the sun went down, we ate a sandwich, watched the stars come out, smoked a joint, had some cookies, and got into our sleeping bags while we listened to my one-speaker cassette player and one of my favorite albums, Jimi Hendrix's *Are You Experienced*.

Donna and I had the same brand and model sleeping bag and I was able to zip my bag up to hers, which was fantastic, at least at first. We started making out but, when one thing led to another, she stopped me again. I asked her why and she finally opened up to me.

"Ken, after I invited you down, I found out I was pregnant and, early this morning, I went to have an abortion. I didn't know it would mess up my mind this much." Of all the things Donna might have said, I'd never seen *that* coming. "I'm so sorry to be in this state of mind and, to be honest, what I'd like to do is go back to L.A. tomorrow morning. How about I come up to San Francisco next weekend and I'm sure I'll be ready to have a really good time with you then?"

I would've been a heartless bastard to have done anything but agree.

The next morning, we were driving toward the coast and we came to the turn off for highway 5 going north. Donna suddenly pulled off. "I think you'll have an easier time hitching a ride from here back to San Francisco than you would in Orange County. I'll see you next Friday." She dropped me off right there.

I waited a while, a little stunned at the way the weekend had turned out, and finally a VW van stopped and picked me up. The driver, a big guy with long hair and a beard, said, "I'm heading to Yosemite where I was a few days ago with my girlfriend and a bunch of friends. While I was there, I fell while driving my Harley and messed it up so much I couldn't drive it anymore. I hitched back to South California to get my van to put my broken bike in for the ride home. There's gonna be a big party at our campsite tonight and you're welcome to join us."

I was pretty pumped up to join a bunch of people and a party in Yosemite. This was going to be a great night after all. The guy had a fridge in the van, filled with cold beer, and we drank one after the other for the ride up there. I was pretty drunk when we entered Yosemite in the high country around Crane Flats.

All of a sudden, the guy decided he was going to drop me off, right there. My invite to the party rescinded without any further discussion. This really wasn't turning out to be a great weekend.

I got out and there I was at 7,000 ft. elevation, on the side of a road, in heavy forest, and the sun was going down fast. I tried hitching for a while but there weren't many cars going by and it was getting cold. I laid my sleeping bag out on the side of the road and got into it. At least I was warm in there. I saw lights heading my way and thought I'd give it one more try.

I got up quickly, held out my thumb, and, voilà, a cool 280 SL Mercedes screeched to a stop. "I'm going to Berkeley," the driver told me, "so if that works for you, I could take you all the way there." That sounded great as I knew I could stay the night in my old fraternity, Sigma Chi, for free and then head back to the city in the morning. I did just that. What a nice guy and great car. I finally got lucky.

*****

The following Friday, sure enough Donna called. "I'm on my way and I'll be in the city by late afternoon." When she arrived, I met her and had her follow me to the place I was living with my friend, John, up in Twin Peaks. He had what used to be a construction management office, a one-story, cheaply made place that, when they were done with it, made for a two-bedroom, one-bath abode with a small kitchen and living room. It was flimsy but just fine for John and, when I'd moved in right after my wife left me, he let me sleep on his couch.

John's place was just down the street on Grandview, right below Market Street. It was way up in the hills and had a great view of San Francisco, the Bay bridge, and the Berkeley and Oakland Hills. Donna and I came back and John had his girlfriend over. We sat around for a few hours, partying, and then they retired to his room while I laid the couch cushions together on the floor as I thought it might give a little more elbow room without the back of the couch impeding us.

Donna and I went at each other like gangbusters, making up for the previous weekend's abstinence. She was fantastic. She'd driven all the way up that day and was a dynamo in the sack. Afterwards, we were lying there getting our second wind when John came in. "How about we trade partners?" he asked. I'd always thought John's girlfriend was amazing and here he was offering her up for a shot at Donna. Fortunately, Donna was game and so we did the switch and the night was just wonderful. I don't think I had enough of those nights in my life but the ones I did have sure stood out.

The weekend was a total winner and, when Donna left, I told her I'd love to visit her when I came home from my trip. Two days later, I got a call from her. "Ken, guess what? I quit my job today and I'm going to go to Europe with you."

Gulp, I wasn't ready for that. "Donna, I had a great time with you and really would like to see you again but I want to travel alone. You should go back to your boss and try to smooth things out and get your job back." I never saw her again.

*****

Just a week before I left for London, I received another phone call. It was Suzy, my ex-wife. "Ken, I knew for weeks that you were leaving the country but knowing you were still here made me feel OK. Now I know you're leaving really soon's made me have second thoughts about not being

4

with you anymore. How about we meet at Henry Africa's on Van Ness Avenue?"

That was something else I didn't see coming. I met Suzy there and it was like a dream come true. I was ecstatic. I loved her so much and my heart soared, knowing we might get back together. We sat in a booth way in the back of the place where we were pretty much out of sight of the few late-afternoon patrons. We ordered a drink and I floated on air as Suzy told me she'd missed me and was thinking long and hard about getting back together with me.

We embraced in the booth and started making out passionately for the first time in many months. I held Suzy so close I wanted to get into her. I kept smelling her hair and trying to soak in every detail about her, mentally revisiting many of the great times we'd had together in the past. It was an impossibly great feeling. Maybe the highest high I've ever felt. I couldn't believe it was true, us getting back together.

"I want to go with you on this trip," Suzy said. I was reeling, thinking about us together, having a whole set of new experiences on the road.

"I have to leave in a week, baby, because I have a ticket that's non-refundable. It's not a regular scheduled flight but a charter. Take some money out of your account and get a ticket to London. I'll wait for you to arrive, no matter how long it takes."

Somewhere along the way, a shred of doubt crept into Suzy's mind and, just like that, she started having doubts about leaving the asshole she left me for. It was just a slight hesitation but, right then and there, I knew I'd lost her again. I got up from the table, shattered emotionally, and blurted out, with tears streaming down my face, "Go fuck yourself," and walked out of the place with several people turning to see who said that and to whom.

I was in a daze as I walked down Van Ness Avenue to Market Street, past a group of hard-core-looking guys who started to hassle me. Not using my head, I just barked insanely at them and they all parted and let me continue on my way. I was out of it for a couple of hours before I realized how crazy I was to yell at those guys and how lucky I was to still be in one piece.

On the way home, all I could think of, besides my grief, was the song my wife dedicated to me not that long before we split up — "Lean on Me" by Bill Withers. How ironic. I certainly wasn't able to lean on her anymore. The next week couldn't go fast enough for me. I wanted a change of scenery. Badly.

*****

5

I boarded the aircraft. My seat was near the window in the first row with the bulkhead directly in front. In the middle was a nerdy-looking guy and in the aisle seat was a very good-looking young woman about my age. The stewardess came around after take-off, pouring drinks. Unlike the major airlines and their 2 oz. bottles of various types of alcohol, this charter flight was pouring drinks into 8 oz. glasses from quarts of booze. I hadn't really been into drinking spirits that much during those heavy psychedelic years but, when in Rome... I ordered Chivas on the rocks. The stewardess must have poured me 6 oz. of the stuff, almost filling the water glass.

The guy in the middle asked for some juice and the young lady in the aisle seat, following my lead, asked for Chivas too. She and I bonded fairly quickly, partly because we were getting plastered from our drinks. She told me her name was Daniela and she was going to meet her penpal, Christina, who was coming down from Liverpool to meet her at Luton airport.

The meal came and, by the time we'd finished eating, the guy in the middle was becoming a major obstacle for us. "Hey, Barney, my friend, how about letting the young lady sit in the middle so we can talk a little more easily?" I asked. He was all too happy to oblige, much to my good fortune. I might not have been so eager to trade places if I was in his shoes.

Now that she and I were close together, the chemistry really took hold. The meal trays were removed and the lights were lowered in the plane. We took one of the flimsy blankets and put it over our laps and proceeded to make out. We were all over each other and really making a scene.

Flash to the next morning. We were still approaching London when she said, "Hey, guys, how would you both like to come with me and Christina back to Liverpool and spend time together?"

"Sounds good to me," said Barney who was also traveling alone.

"I'm up for it! I've nothing much planned," I told her. In all honesty, I just wanted to do the easiest thing possible as I was suffering with a pretty nasty hangover. I figured I'd just go with her plan and keep it simple. After we arrived and checked in through customs, we found Christina. We had our luggage — well, backpacks — and I asked Christina, "Where did you park your car?"

"I took a bus down here," she replied. "Let's see what the bus schedule looks like for the return trip." We checked and the next bus didn't leave for six hours. Nobody wanted to wait.

"Why don't we rent a car?" Christina suggested. "But I have to admit I don't drive." In fact, I was the only one with a driver's license and so we took a rental car in Christina's name but with me listed as the driver. Before that day, I'd never driven a car with a stick shift that you had to use your left hand on. Not only that, but the steering wheel was on the right side and the cars were driving on the opposite side of the street from where they drive in America. While feeling in tip-top shape, this task would have been hard enough, near impossible, on the first attempt but, with a hangover like I had, it was the Twilight Zone.

I drove out of the airport slowly, gingerly, not gaining much speed and already horns were honking. The rest of my fellow passengers couldn't care less. They were yapping away and having a jolly good time while I was sweating bullets. And that was before I got to the first roundabout. Who in God's heaven invented roundabouts? What kind of masochist thought that one up? It must have been an engineer with Nostradamus-type powers, figuring some day an American with a hangover will come, so we'll make it as hard as humanly possible for him to survive long enough to make it to his destination.

I had to go around and around that first roundabout at least three or four times before being able to figure out how to get out of it and continue on my way. It seemed like every quarter mile there was another one and another one. After about six of them, I drove back the other way.

"Everyone, quiet down. Daniela, Barney, and Christina, I have an announcement to make. I'm taking you back to the airport. Here's $20 for gas. I'm getting the tube into London. Nice knowing you."

Just like that, I got out and waved goodbye. I have no idea what they did with the car.

LONDON AND ONWARDS

After dropping out of the ride to Christina's home with my new-found friends, I headed down the elevator at Luton station to an underground subway for the very first time. There was a large map on the wall showing the different lines and I started searching for the inevitable "you are here." A young girl, probably no more than thirteen, saw me searching the map and asked if I needed any assistance. When I nodded yes, she pointed out where we were and asked where I'd like to go. I chose Kensington and eventually got on the train.

When it reached my station, I was very hungry. I found a small market and took my purchase to a park nearby. After eating, I walked and walked and finally found a pub that looked inviting. I put my pack down and started drinking warm beer. It took a little getting used to but not that long. I had a great time there and ate one of the meat and potato turnovers that I soon discovered seemed to be in every pub. *I could live on those, no problem*, I thought.

After leaving, I wasn't in the mood to search for a hostel so I stayed in part of Hyde Park which was very close by. I was pretty wet when I awoke the next morning. I shook off the cobwebs and tried to find the nearest hostel. You have to remember this was before the days of mobile phones and Google's help. Several hours later, I finally found a cool-looking hostel. I went in and they told me that, without a reservation, I had no chance of getting a room. Sorry.

I was still damp and the weather was miserable. I decided to leave the UK, right then and there. I asked someone which direction to Dover. I wasn't a very seasoned traveler yet and didn't even have the foresight to buy a travel guide before leaving home. I'd gone into a bookstore earlier and found I could get a ferry from Dover to either Calais, in France, or Ostende, Belgium. I hitch-hiked all day long and finally reached Dover after at least ten rides. My favorite was when the driver let me off right outside the walls of Canterbury. That gave me a little shiver up and down my spine remembering *Canterbury Tales* from school days.

One thing I noticed wherever I went was how different people sounded from each other. Some of the drivers were very easy to understand but others had incredibly thick accents. I kept thinking, *These people are speaking English and I have no idea what they're saying*. It was pretty strange.

In Dover, I went to the ticket office and the next ferry out was to Ostende that evening. It was already late afternoon so I took the boat, had a couple of beers, found a good chair, and tried to go to sleep. That wasn't easy as there was a huge contingent of Germans on holiday and they were doing the bunny hop around the boat for hours, singing wildly, while drunk as hell. The line of them stretched all around the boat. Ninety percent of them had a fifth of booze in one hand. I had to hand it to them, they certainly took advantage of any situation to have a good time.

The boat pulled into Ostende around 1:30 a.m. As I walked off the ferry, the visibility was very poor with a thick fog blanketing the town. I had no idea where I was in relation to places to stay so I went down under the boardwalk, onto the sand, where I was protected somewhat from the dampness and got into my sleeping bag to sleep.

I awoke to the sounds of boat motors and a bright blue sky. Walking up onto the street, I noticed hundreds of people on bicycles going about their business. The commuters were mostly cyclists, not motorists. I walked around the town, where the scene was the same, enjoying how quiet it was yet still busy.

I found a place selling sandwiches with maybe two slices of salami on a long dry roll but figured I'd better enjoy whatever I could get. I knew Belgium was near the Netherlands so I set Amsterdam to be my destination. I managed to hitch a couple of rides that took me to a highway heading in the right direction. My problem with getting rides was I had a very large backpack and the majority of cars were tiny so getting my pack into them wasn't the easiest of chores. A couple of potential rides actually changed their minds while I was trying to force my pack into the car.

After my second ride, I was just off the highway on a frontage road in farmland. I spent several hours in the same spot because of a lack of traffic. It was in the days before plastic bottles of water and I was getting pretty thirsty. A truck came by and made a hard turn onto the on ramp of the highway and, from the top of a mountain of potatoes the truck was hauling, four or five of them fell onto the street, not far away from where I was. I went over and picked up a couple.

I had a pretty lousy boy scout knife with me and the blade wasn't very sharp but it was fine cutting a potato. The first few bites were great and I convinced myself I was enjoying it but, by the time I finished a whole potato, I came to the conclusion raw potatoes left a lot to be desired.

The next ride was the one I was waiting for and took me all the way to Amsterdam where the driver dropped me off at Dam Square. When I got out, I saw a bunch of people sitting at the base of the national monument. They looked a lot like the hippies back home. *Ah*, I thought, *I've made it to my kind of place*. There were people smoking hashish and others selling it. I could hear the sounds of Led Zeppelin and Mott the Hoople seemingly coming out of thin air as I walked around the area.

Sleeping bags were strewn everywhere but I'd already slept outdoors the first two nights of my trip and really wanted to find a real bed and a shower. Someone pointed out a street leading away from the square and said to just go find any bar as they all had dormitory rooms up above. I did just that and it worked out very well. The first guy I met upstairs in the dorm room told me I had to be careful because people had had their packs stolen. He had an extra bike lock he loaned me for the night.

I headed downstairs to the bar to get a beer and a sandwich. People were smoking dope, cutting lines of cocaine, right on the top of the bar, and I realized this was one special city. I always thought San Francisco was loose but Amsterdam topped it by far. The party was really taking off, great music was playing, and everyone was very generous with their drugs with joints and chillums being passed around. (A chillum is a pipe that's held vertically in your hand and you smoke it by pressing your lips to your fingers formed in a particular way. And then suck. Can't forget the sucking in of the smoke.) I finally couldn't take any more and went upstairs to turn in for the night.

Next day, the guy who lent me his bike lock told me about a tour at the Heineken brewery. We went over there and started the tour at 10 a.m. After an hour, we were in a room with long tables where waitresses poured beer as fast as you could drink it. Not a great idea to drink a lot of beer on an empty stomach. The tour was over at noon and I was retching into a planter bed shortly after. I went straight back to the dormitory room to sleep it off.

That night, I had a big meal and started partying again in the bar. I noticed a tall, gorgeous brunette dancing behind me and, on a couple of occasions, our eyes met. I felt a tap on my shoulder a little later and it was her. I turned around and she asked me, "Do you believe in love at first sight?" with the sweetest voice imaginable. She said her name was Riet then she asked me, "Would you like a hash brownie?"

"I sure would."

"The brownies are at my apartment so, if you have anything upstairs, go get it and come with me."

I went up, got my backpack, and we walked a few blocks to her apartment. It was just a dream night. She was clearly a prophet because I was in love with her at first sight. I just didn't know her thoughts would be reciprocal. We spent the whole of the next day at her place. She cooked for me, we showered together, got high, and made love. I never wanted to leave

11

that apartment again.

The next morning, she must have gotten up early because she gently shook me awake and was all dressed and looking fantastic. She kissed me, told me I could stay, the key was on the kitchen table, and she'd be back from Rotterdam in a day or so. She didn't come back the next day and, on the afternoon of the second day, I was walking by the American Express office, which in the '70s was a major meeting place for travelers. I saw a flyer on the wall that was looking for riders in a large van to share gas to drive to Barcelona. They would be leaving the following morning.

I really wanted to be with Riet but I felt funny just sitting around waiting, without knowing for how long. At the last minute the next morning, I wrote a note to Riet telling her I loved our time together and then hurried to meet the people at American Express. They had one of those old Metro vans. It looked like the big bread trucks that companies used to deliver bread in my neighborhood when I was really young; sometimes they'd give you one of their sugar donuts if they were in a good mood.

Nine of us piled into the van. It was crowded but the American couple who organized the whole thing had a hookah up front with four long tubes coming from it for those in back to puff away on. We also had quite a few bottles of cheap red wine so we were set.

We made it as far as Lille in France the first day. The American couple were from California and there was another guy from Los Angeles. He told me he'd traveled all the way from London to Kabul, Afghanistan, before coming back to Europe. A month of that time he was traveling with a few other people on horseback. He'd quit his job as an accountant and started his travels in Europe and kept drifting further east. He showed me his passport picture which looked like a different guy. He said he'd lost 70 lbs since he started traveling and was very fit for the first time since his early twenties.

The first night, we parked in a field in Lille. Everyone slept outside except for the guy from L.A. and a very cute buxom lady from Denmark, named Hannah. Before we left the next day, he told me it was really cold inside the van and with his summer sleeping bag he couldn't sleep outside. I told him I'd like to have a shot sleeping inside the van if Hannah slept in there again and, if she did, I'd trade him my goose down bag for his for the night. I just wanted to have a shot at Hannah.

After eating a morning meal, we bought lots of bottles of wine and took off for Paris. We were drinking the wine and smoking the hookah of hashish and having a grand time. After a couple of hours, the guy from L.A. realized he'd left his leather jacket at a gas station in Lille. So, we turned around and drove back. This guy really had his tail between his legs from causing us to lose so much time.

12

Finally, we were once again heading south toward Paris. We arrived in the late afternoon, really, really wasted. We found a market next to a parking lot and several of us went and peed against a wall while the rush-hour cars slowly inched by, honking at us, knowing what we were doing against that wall. The other passengers went straight into the market.

When I finished, I went into the store to find something good to eat that we could all share and I noticed a couple of the people shoving food inside their clothes and then purchasing other stuff. So, we all bought some food and at the same time stole other stuff to make for a huge feast once we got outside of Paris into another field where we could park, feast, and sleep.

That evening, to my total delight, Hannah climbed into the van when everyone was setting up their sleeping bags outside. I traded my bag, like I'd promised, with the guy from L.A., climbed into the van with Hannah, and lay down next to her. I was full of wine and high with anticipation of things that might happen. We started cuddling and then making out. This was going way better than I'd figured it would.

The L.A. guy had told me she was a cold fish the night before but I found Hannah to be a very enthusiastic kisser. I tried to take it to the next level but that was as far as I was to get. She said, "Ken, I like you, but I have a boyfriend who I'm going to meet in Barcelona."

I thought to myself, *If you don't tell, Hannah, I won't.*

"I don't mind kissing," she added, "which to me is just being friendly, but don't expect anything more as I love my boyfriend."

I dozed off. Several hours later, I woke up, no longer warm from the wine and shivering from the cold. The guy was right. I think the metal walls of the van actually made it colder inside than it was outside. I'm sure that anyone who knows science would shoot holes in my theory but I was freezing my balls off. I think my teeth were even chattering.

Hannah woke up and heard and felt me shaking. "Ken, come close to me." She pulled my face right into her bosom and then put my hands together, palm to palm, and placed them way up between her upper thighs. "You'll be OK now. Sleep," and she kissed me on my forehead. I did eventually fall back asleep but for a good amount of time I was very excited and had to tell myself to calm down or I'd end up with blue balls. All in all, I did greatly appreciate the survival skills demonstrated by this Danish girl.

*****

Also in the van was a guy named Tony who was from Toronto. He had long black hair halfway down his back and he loved shooting photos of everything. He'd just hold his camera as we were cruising down the road,

13

aiming it out the large front windows of the van. While still in Belgium, he was aiming it with his big telephoto lens and clicking off very fast shots. Suddenly, a car way up in front of us swerved, rolled, and flew high into the air before coming down on its roof off the side of the highway. Our van driver just drove on by.

When we got to Spain, Tony had the photos developed and his contact sheet showed the car in mid-air, upside down. In today's digital world, that shot could have been emailed to a news agency for some instant cash.

The other passenger that stands out in my mind was a young guy from Glasgow. I never understood anything he said except for one phrase — "You got a face like a kipper." He must have said it ten times a day, to everyone, everywhere, and we all just laughed each time. He was a tough-looking young guy and especially fond of whatever alcohol we had, which was mostly red wine.

On the third day, we stopped in Carcassonne, a hilltop medieval citadel. We drove in a pretty flat area for hours and in the distance we saw a small hill. As we got closer to it, we realized there was a castle on the hill. It was really a spectacular sight to see from afar and even better as we got closer. We stopped to walk around the streets of the castle as it was too beautiful to bypass completely. If we hadn't been hell-bent on making it to Barcelona, it would have been a great place to stay overnight.

That night, we stopped at the border with Spain and had to show our passports to the border guards. It seemed strange there were guards at all as there weren't any going from Belgium into the Netherlands or into France. Not only did they want to see our passports but they wanted to see how much money we had, whether cash or traveler's checks. Everyone passed the test except for our "face like a kipper" friend. He had a total of $7 on him and they took him out of the van and told us to be on our way.

I have no clue what happened to him but I'm betting he didn't make it into Spain.

SPAIN

After crossing the border, we continued on and, at a very late hour, pulled into Arenys De Mar and found a hotel. As it turned out, we'd picked a great place in town which faced the square and the Mediterranean beyond. The rooms were cheap and clean and there was a restaurant downstairs. Tony and I shared a comfortable room with two double beds.

If we wanted to go into Barcelona, it was just a ten-minute ride by train and the station was just across the street from the square. Not really a station, just a small platform where you'd stand and wait. The weather was very mild and most days were good beach days, not at all cold like Amsterdam was in late September.

Right around the corner from the hotel was a wine shop and the favorite choice for the budget travelers was the three-liter bottle of a good, dry red wine that was placed into a plastic bucket. I guess they did that in case those drinking from it started getting slippery fingers after consuming the first two liters.

Most restaurants in town allowed people to bring their wine with them when they dined. Tony and I were midway through our three-liter bottle one night and sat down in our hotel restaurant to have some dinner. Just as we ordered, two beautiful women with long, almost to the waist, light brown hair, walked in and in about two seconds I realized I was seeing double. Twins! Dressed just the same. They sat at a table close to the door with two empty tables between us. The food came from the kitchen for them and us at about the same time. For a while before the food came, the one facing me kept glancing up and we smiled back and forth a couple of times. While we were eating, we kept making eye contact. It reminded me of a scene in the movie *Tom Jones* when Tom and a woman had a similar moment while eating and the looks the two of them gave one another, while food was sliding down the chin, was X-rated, if a smile could be considered so.

I couldn't take it anymore. This was too good an opportunity. I got up and went over to their table. "Good evening, ladies. How would you like to join us at our table?" They grabbed their plates and followed me. Tony and I sat on one side, across from the two of them, with the one I was playing

15

the smiling game with directly across from me. Her name was Janie. They were from Australia and had a VW bug rental car and were driving around Europe together.

Janie offered, "We've been camping out most of our trip but decided to get a room for a night and spoil ourselves." We continued to eat and drink and things were going very well. After dinner, Janie asked, "Would you guys like to come up to our room for a nightcap?" Of course we wanted to go up to their room. How sweet that they offered. When we'd settled in, Janie and I sat on one bed and Tony and Janie's sister on the other. The beds were parallel to one another, just a couple of feet apart. The lamp in the room wasn't all that strong but there was a street light directly in front of their window so the room had the benefit of that extra light. We had lots of laughs and talked about things in common with Australia, Canada, and the USA.

We finally ran out of things to talk about. Janie got a little closer and that was all I needed. I grabbed hold of her and we started making out and, within a minute or two, she tore off her dress. I undressed quickly and we were all over each other with a vengeance. We did it on the bed, off the bed, half on and half off, sideways, probably upside down, and anything else under the sun.

As I mentioned, the room was pretty lit up and every now and then I'd glance over to the other bed and there were Tony and Janie's sister not doing anything. They were sitting in what looked like stunned silence. That didn't matter one bit to Janie or me. We just kept going and finally dropped to the bed, sweating and exhausted, and instantly passed out. I remember waking up with the two of us still clinging to one another. It was dark, maybe three or four in the morning.

"Janie, I'm going back down to my room."

"OK, Ken. Come to the beach around nine or ten and my sister and I will cook breakfast for you and Tony."

I let myself out and went down to my room. I woke up around nine to the sound of Tony showering. I sat on the side of the bed, waiting for my turn in the shower. When he came out, he said, "Ken, thanks for the amazing show."

I broke out laughing. "Tony, what in the world were you just sitting there for? You two should have joined in."

"I tried, brother, but she kept pushing me away. Anyway, watching you and Janie was just mind-blowing."

Either she wasn't that into him or she was just enjoying watching me and her sister going at it. I don't know. Shortly after, he and I found the girls on the beach and they cooked a superior meal from scratch, just with their camping gear. Janie looked great in the sunlight. She sure made me forget Riet and how depressed I was over my wife leaving me.

Janie took me aside. "My sister and I have been having a fight this morning."

"About what?"

"I told her I want you to come with us the rest of our trip and she complained we don't have that much room."

That sure sounds like a great idea, I thought.

"We decided to sleep on it and make our decision tomorrow."

That night there was a big party at one of the restaurants in town. It had a large dance floor and live music to dance to. Tony and I met Janie and her sister at the restaurant. Janie looked like she'd just stepped out of a magazine. Elegant. Gorgeous. She could stop traffic, she was so beautiful. She looked way too good for me to be with. I didn't have much in the way of evening clothing so was wearing jeans and one of those blue work shirts that had an embroidered Yosemite Sam on the back of the shirt. Oh, and a Tweetie Pie on the front pocket. Not exactly a dazzling outfit for clubbing in Europe.

When Tony and I walked in, there was a Spanish guy standing at the table, leaning in close to Janie and talking to her. He looked like he belonged. He was probably local and even I had to admit to myself he looked more like her match. I didn't let on that I was thinking that though.

I sat down next to Janie and we silently nursed our drinks. Eventually I asked, "Well, did you and your sister decide on taking me with you guys?"

"So sorry, Ken, my sister wouldn't give in. I'm pretty disappointed but we set out to do this trip on our own and that's how it's gonna end."

Dinner came and we had more drinks and finally I was feeling no pain. The sharp-looking Spanish guy came over and asked Janie to dance. Now, feeling the alcohol, I was getting more than a little peed off. They got up and danced and, to me, it looked way too intimate. I was starting to boil. They stayed on the floor and had another dance. I thought to myself, *That's enough of this*, got up, walked over, and tapped the guy on the shoulder, wanting to cut in. "I'd like to dance with Janie, please."

He ignored me. I tapped again and again he ignored me. I then took him by the arm and pulled him away from her. He tripped and went down. Two of his friends came over and the three of them grabbed me and pulled me out the front door and into the street where they proceeded to kick my butt. I ended up on the ground and curled up. There were several more kicks and I was hurt. In more ways than one.

"Ken, again you put on a good show," Tony told me. "But not the one I was hoping for." He gave me a good teasing for days. The girls had taken off and the rest of the time there I avoided going to dances. We did a few day trips into Barcelona, seeing all the amazing Gaudí architecture, which was incredible. The Basilica of the Sagrada Família, which should be finished in time for the centenary of Gaudí's death in 2026, looked stunning even back then. We enjoyed wandering round the Gothic quarter and down La Ramba, Barcelona's most famous street which stretches for over a mile, all the way down to the sea. But finally, we'd had enough of Arenys De Mar. It was time to move on.

*****

Tony and I took a train to Malaga on the Costa Del Sol. Lots of great beaches down there. We boarded the train in Barcelona and each bought a couple of bottles of wine for the overnight train. We had a sleeper car where we met an English guy who'd just finished working on a winery in France. He said we should go to the bar and have a few pops from his bottles of cognac. The winery had given him two as a little bonus when he left. We sat in the bar car, passing the bottle back and forth, getting pretty blasted. I was unaware, with my limited experience with alcohol at that point in my life, that cognac was the same alcohol content as whiskey. I was mostly into weed and psychedelics. My brothers and sisters all looked down on alcohol, as did I.

So, here we were in the bar car, eating snacks and drinking cognac and wine before eventually making it back to our compartment. On one side of the compartment was the English guy on the bottom bunk, with me in the middle one and Tony up on top. Already in their births and drinking wine were two ladies and a guy, all speaking Spanish.

"*Buenas noches*," they said and immediately offered us each a cup of wine. We took them up on their offer. The two women were pretty young and attractive. After several more cups of wine, we were all having a lot of laughs, despite us speaking English and them only Spanish, which none of us understood. The English guy said to the other side, "You ladies are very hot," and we laughed. They joined in. One of the girls said something in Spanish and the three of them broke out laughing which prompted another line by Tony who escalated the tone of the conversation, saying, "Lady, I bet you would look great without that nightgown." We broke out laughing and they did too after a moment.

They replied with something in Spanish and pretty soon the lines from us were just downright X-rated but they kept coming back at us, seemingly tit for tat. Finally, we all tired, turned out the lights, and went to sleep. In the morning, we knew we weren't far from arriving, not in Malaga, like we'd originally thought, but in Córdoba, which was still a distance from

18

Malaga. I guess we made a mistake purchasing the ticket because we were told we'd have to get off in Córdoba.

We noticed people walking in the corridor with soap, towel, and toothbrushes so we also got up and went to freshen up. When I came out of the bathroom, the Spanish girl, who was on the top berth across from Tony, was passing by me. She stopped and said, "Man, that sure was fun last night."

I turned purple. "You speak English?"

"We all speak English. We're Americans going to school in Barcelona."

We both broke out laughing helplessly.

*****

Tony and I had a cup of coffee in Córdoba but really wanted to be at the beach again so took a train down there that same day. We stayed in a small hotel near Torremolinos, a town that James Michener wrote a book about, which was where the action was. I even read his *The Drifters* while hanging on that beach. Seemed like the right book to read while drifting around Europe.

We hung there on the beach for a few days, often in a café which had a jukebox. I was in a playful mood there one time, found the Beatles' "Revolution 9" on it and put in enough money to play it ten times in a row. Then I left the café. For a lot of people, even devout Beatle fans, this song isn't easy to listen to. *Karma will get me for this*, I thought as I left the café.

One morning, Tony asked me, "Ken, you want to go see a bullfight today?"

"Uh, no thanks. You go and have a good time. I'll hang here." I had no interest in seeing a bull get butchered to the sound of screaming crowds. I hung out on the beach religiously. There was a disco there we went to a couple of nights but we didn't meet any ladies and the fact that cool weather was following us helped us decide we needed to get down to Morocco where there were lots of good beaches and hashish.

The next morning, we took a bus to Algeciras, a port in southern Spain. It turned out it was Ramadan. I really knew nothing about Ramadan except that it was a month long and Muslims didn't eat during the day. When we boarded the bus, the majority of the passengers were wearing a fez, the kind of hat you see Shriners, or Shrine Masons, wearing. But it was clear to me that Shriners weren't the same as these guys. They weren't American for a start.

We pulled out of the bus station on a beautiful, crystal-clear morning

19

and drove along the coast, high up on a bluff much of the time which offered wide, open views of the Mediterranean and sometimes beaches below. The only problem was the guy in front of me pulled the shade down, covering the window and hiding the view. After a few moments, I made the shade go back up and settled in to enjoy the beautiful view again. Once again, he closed the shade. Now it was a battle of wills. We went up and down a couple more times and I finally lost my temper, grabbed the fez off his head, and tossed it up past him a few rows toward the front of the bus.

He turned around, jumped over the seat, and we wrestled a little, no punches. Tony and a couple of the guys with fezzes jumped in and broke up our struggles. My adversary moved up toward the front and the next guy in his seat left the shade open. I didn't realize how stupid a move it was on my part. I had no way of knowing back then that he was Muslim and that they fasted and often slept during the daylight hours of Ramadan. It's only in retrospect that I know I made a lot of mistakes while traveling. Thankfully, I survived them.

*****

When we reached Algeciras, we purchased tickets for the ferry the following day. That afternoon, we met some people from California who were also taking the ferry the next day to Ceuta with us. One of them was a cute, size-one blonde who latched onto me. She said over a couple of glasses of wine, "Ken, it would be great if you could pretend you are my boyfriend when we get to Morocco as I'm a little scared being on my own there."

That night, we slept together so I guess I didn't really have to play act. I was sort of a boyfriend even if I only knew her for 24 hours. She was with a couple and another single woman. We all got on the ferry together and set out across the seas. Once we landed, the ladies went down the ramp first and then the guys. The customs guy said to us, "No entry, unless you cut your hair."

Tony and I had long hair, as did the other guy. Tony pulled out some scissors. "Here, Ken, cut my hair. I really want to go to Morocco." I proceeded to cut Tony's hair all the way around and just above the ears. Tony then cut the other guy's hair. They both looked really bad.

I changed my mind. I didn't want to cut my hair. "You know, guys, it was fun, but I'm going back to Spain. No chance I'm cutting my hair."

They all got off the ferry, including my one-day girlfriend, and I sailed back across the water to Algeciras. I ended up taking a bus back to Malaga and then getting a flight from there to Madrid and a flight to Rome. A whole new adventure was about to happen.

ITALY AND GREECE

I landed in Rome and asked the taxi driver to take me to an inexpensive hotel. A *pensione*. He pulled up in front of a pretty nice-looking place and I told him, "I don't have any lira so let me cash a traveler's check inside while I register."

"That's OK," he said, "you owe me $20." I signed my name on the $50 traveler's check and set about signing into the hotel registry. When I'd done so, I turned around, noticing the taxi driver was gone, and asked the receptionist, "Did you change my traveler's check yet?"

"Yes, I put $50 worth of lira on the counter and the driver took it all. I figured that was what you owed him."

He was gone. I was visibly upset at getting ripped off as I started my time in a new place. The bellman showed me to my room and, a minute after he left, my phone started ringing. I picked it up and a woman's voice said, "Mr. Liss, I'm a guest here and I was having a drink in the lobby, not far from the desk. I heard what happened with that taxi driver. If you feel like it, why don't you come down and I'll buy you a drink and show you not all Italians are bad people."

Downstairs I went. I walked toward the lobby and there was an older woman, maybe 40, a redhead, looking very attractive. Being a youngster of 24, she seemed old to me but certainly not too old to have a drink with. I sat down and she ordered a drink for me. We sat and talked and talked. She said she was from just outside Florence but in Rome on business, leaving the following morning for home which was a villa in the Tuscan hills.

"How would you like to come with me tomorrow and be my guest at the villa? I have lots of very interesting friends and we all socialize quite a bit. I think you'd enjoy them and I know they would enjoy you."

I looked at the way she was dressed and responded, "You know, I'm a very devout budget traveler and, looking at you, I think I would feel out of place being with your friends, looking like a typical hippie traveler."

"Don't give it a second thought," she said. "When we get back, I'll take you shopping and buy you a whole new wardrobe. No strings attached. Stay as long as you like." Finally, she added, "You don't have to make up your mind right now. Think about it tonight and, if you decide you'd like to take

23

me up on my offer, be here in the lobby tomorrow morning at 9 a.m. It's up to you."

I did give it a lot of thought and, in the end, I didn't meet her the next morning. Do I regret my decision? Yes, I do. It would have been an adventure and who knows what might have come of it?

*****

After a few days in Rome, I met some Canadians from British Columbia as I walked the Spanish Steps connecting the lower Piazza di Spagna with the upper Piazza Trinità dei Monti and its beautiful twin tower church that dominates the skyline. We partied throughout the night. The Canadians were a couple and a single lady who was rather quiet but seemed pleasant enough and we seemed to hit it off, even if it was me who did all the talking.

The guy said, "Ken, we're taking a train tomorrow morning way down south to Brindisi and, from there, we're going to get a ferry the following evening, an overnighter, stopping in Corfu and then continuing on to Patras, Greece. Would you like to join us?"

"Sure, I'm game. I have no real plans."

The next morning, I met them at the station. People kept warning me to pay attention to the gypsies that infiltrated the place. They were there for one thing only — to rip off tourists. I managed to keep them at bay. The Canadians all wore maple-leaf patches on their clothes and backpacks to make sure no one mistook them for being Americans. Americans didn't seem to have a problem being outed as Americans but Canadians found that to be something horrible, thus the maple-leaf patches.

We shared a train compartment down to Brindisi. On the train, I pulled out my cassette player and played Cream's "Traintime" off their *Wheels of Fire* album. It became a tradition with me whenever I'd take a train anywhere. In the years after, I added "Runaway Train" by Soul Asylum, "Speed Kills" by Ten Years After, and "Station Man" by Fleetwood Mac. Can't ever have too much good music.

We got into Brindisi pretty late. We stayed overnight in a hostel and that quiet lady and I had a roll in the hay even with people sleeping in beds nearby in the dorm room. The next day, we hung out in the city until around 4 p.m. when we walked over to the port. The ferry wasn't supposed to leave until 7 p.m. The Canadians figured being there early would ensure a good seat. I sat with them, waiting for a couple of hours.

The single Canadian girl was starting to get attached to me and was pretty upset when I walked off to check out the ever-growing group of travelers who were also waiting for the ferry. While walking around the crowd, I met a very cute lady from Boulder, Colorado, in the Rocky Mountains, named Sarah. We really hit it off.

When the ferry came, it was obvious there was a ton of room on the boat for everyone. It was like a party for the first four or five hours. There were plenty of reclining seats and bars upstairs and downstairs and so many people to see and get to know. I sat with the Canadians who weren't into that scene. They sat and drank beers in a low-key manner while the party was raging on not far away.

After a couple of hours, I couldn't contain myself and I joined in with the festivities, connecting with Sarah again. We danced and had a really great time together. When it was time to sleep, I went back to the Canadians as I knew their low-energy level would put me to sleep. Might as well get a good night's sleep when you can.

In the morning, we pulled into Corfu and a bunch of people got off the ferry and new passengers arrived. I'd heard about Corfu and, for me, it was too far north. I wanted to go to islands much further south, knowing that meant warmer weather.

The ferry finally pulled into Patras around 7 p.m. When we got off, it was chaotic as people formed lines to get on buses that would take us all the way to Athens. I saw Sarah and we decided we wanted to sit together on the bus ride which would get us into Athens around midnight. The Canadians just weren't as much fun. It was a no-brainer to hang out with Sarah.

We got on the next bus out, sat together, and just had the best time. When we pulled into Athens, the two of us started walking down the street, going with the flow of travelers, seeing where they would stay and then making a choice for ourselves. We walked arm in arm, enjoying a beautiful warm night. Out of nowhere, came the Canadian girl. "You are what they're talking about when they talk about an ugly American," she raged. "You are representative of why people around the world hate Americans." With that, she turned and walked after her friends.

Sarah started calling me Ugly Ken after that episode but was still keen to spend the night with me. The next day, she told me she and some friends were going north and I was welcome to join them. I really wanted to head south to some islands and beaches. A big hug later, she was off and I headed to Constitution Square and sat down at one of the chairs there, enjoying the sunshine with a FIX beer.

In Constitution Square, with its fountain in the center and the Tomb of the Unknown Soldier outside the Greek parliament along one side, I just enjoyed the people-watching opportunities. Great comfortable seats and a constant flow of foot traffic. This was just before the '72 elections. On a seat right next to me, was a very attractive brunette.

"Hello, I'm Ken. I'm from San Francisco. What's your name?" I was soon asking her.

"Really, Ken? I'm Paula and I'm also from San Francisco. Which part of the city did you live in?

"Grandview Street. How about you?"

"What a small world. I lived around the corner on Grandview Terrace."

Now that really was a small world encounter.

"So, what's that form you're filling out?"

"My absentee ballot for the upcoming election. I hope we can vote Nixon out."

Paula and I really hit it off.

"Ken, I'm gonna take a ferry to Crete tomorrow. Want to join me?"

"You bet I want to."

Another phase of my travels was about to begin.

CRETE

Paula and I took a ferry from Piraeus, south of Athens, where lots of shipping took place. She had a friend with her but, during the evening, we took some valium she picked up at the pharmacy in Athens and we went down and found a bunch of rooms with bunk beds and went into one. The boat started rocking and rolling because of heavy seas and we were coming onto the valium and trying to take off our clothes but it was hard because we kept losing our balance and banging into the bunk beds. We laughed like crazy and still kept working on getting our clothes off. It was like a slapstick comedy and, when we finally got naked and into one of the bunks, we held each other and laughed with tears coming down our faces. The sex by then was anti-climactic by comparison. We crashed for the night. No one lasts too long when taking valium and booze.

The ferry eventually pulled into Heraklion and Paula and her friend went their own way but I got her contact information for someday in the future when we were both back in San Francisco.

On a side note, two years later, in 1974, I was with a few friends, partying at Harrington's on Front Street on St. Patrick's Day, and afterwards we went to my favorite cheap eatery in Chinatown — Woey Loy Goey restaurant. They had an amazing dish I had every time there — roast pork with cabbage and a wonderful gravy with steamed rice. Not really Chinese food at all but this is what I loved there. I felt a tap on the shoulder. "Hey, Kenny, remember our night on the ferry boat to Crete?" I turned around and it was Paula. I got up to give her a hug and she whispered in my ear, "I have a boyfriend now but I'd like to have one more evening with you. Are you up for that? Just a one nighter again?" I was and we went back to her place and the rest is history. I never saw or heard from her again.

Anyway, back in Heraklion, I went to the American Express office and discovered there was a note from a cousin of mine, Bernie, saying he was there and would see if he could hook up with me. I really was hoping to see him but we didn't manage to connect. He'd been at the Olympic Games in Munich and had traveled slowly down, leaving early, after staying in the Olympic village, living right across from the Israeli team's dorm. He was very depressed after the massacre of the Israeli athletes, having gotten to

27

know some of them pretty well. The Palestinian terrorist group, Black September, had taken eleven Israeli Olympic team members hostage and killed them along with a German police officer in what would later be called the Munich massacre.

After a day in Heraklion, a city that I only remember from the number of pickup trucks I saw filled with slain pigs, I got a bus to Ierapetra, a town on the southeast coast of Crete. It was a beautiful, winding, and twisting ride through and over mountainous terrain to our destination.

On the way down, there were only a half dozen people on the bus and among them were best friends from Vancouver. These guys put on a performance for the ages. They mentioned a comedy troupe called Monty Python's Flying Circus who had a TV show on BBC called "And Now For Something Completely Different." I hadn't heard of them or the show, since we didn't get BBC in America at the time. They were kind enough to enact many of their favorite sketches. These guys had it down with "I'm a lumberjack and I'm OK" and so much more being sung and retold. They must have taken many bus rides before this one. It was about a five-hour ride and it went by very quickly thanks to those Canadians.

When we reached Ierapetra, someone pointed out a house a couple of miles outside of town, situated on a beautiful beach. It was a coarse sand beach but the water was crystal clear and refreshing, especially when we were drinking ouzo and smoking hashish every single day. Anthony, the owner of the place we stayed, rented out several rooms with two or three beds in each. The Canadians and I all moved in. Anthony was a real character and a lot of fun to stay with.

I had a roommate named Timothy Leary from Battle Creek, Michigan. "Not *the* Timothy Leary that made LSD famous?" I asked on meeting him.

"No, definitely not," he laughed, "and I'm a heck of a lot younger than Leary is, if you think about it."

Battle Creek is the city a lot of cereals were made and where you would send two box tops of Cheerios and 25 cents for a submarine you could put baking soda into and watch it dive and then surface in your bathtub.

Timothy was a cool guy and a lot of fun. The first day, he said, "Ken, I just came from Kabul, Afghanistan. Take a look at this souvenir I brought back with me." He went into his backpack and pulled out a chunk of hashish, Afghani Primo, the size of his fist. This particular kind of hashish has always been what I considered the best hashish anywhere. He would break off a piece, put it on a pin, and light it. It would slowly burn with a steady stream of smoke coming off it. We would cool our mouths with locally made ouzo. In that town, you could bring any container you had to the factory where they made the ouzo and they'd fill it for 50 cents. What a great combination ouzo and hashish was.

Many nights, the owner of our house would pass around a hat and we'd all put money in and then he'd go to town, buy a bunch of groceries, and come back and cook for us. We'd all drink beer, retsina wine, which tasted horrible, or ouzo. Timothy would pull out his pin with the hash-smoking and it would be passed around. After all the coughing died down, dinner would be served. Afterwards, our host would play his bouzouki and we'd all dance around, trying to imitate moves he showed us. Night after night, we had great fun and always got crazy when the song "Zorba the Greek" came on.

We'd sit on the beach daily and tell stories. This was around the time Billy Hayes was in prison in Turkey for attempting to smuggle a couple of kilos of hashish onto a flight. They made the movie *Midnight Express* about him. Travelers spread all kinds of rumors about him back then, after talking to anyone who just came back from, or knew someone who was recently in, Turkey.

Tuesday night was sangria night at the local disco. Everyone in our house would walk to the disco, each carrying our own, cup, glass, tumbler, whatever we had. You'd pay a dollar to get in and then they'd fill whatever you brought for no extra charge. This wasn't a scene for amateurs. My first sangria night, I had a plastic tumbler and it held way too much sangria. A bad omen.

It didn't take long to get to know a lot of the people there. After an hour, there were many loud drunks dancing and falling on the dance floor. I remember feeling very hot and so, after several fast dances, I took off my shirt and tossed it, to the cheers of some of the spectators. I danced with Timothy, locking arms as we turned and turned. I felt a little dizzy. I sat down on a folding chair next to the packed dance floor. Then the floor rose up and smashed me in the face and the lights went out.

The next thing I knew, I was behind Anthony on his motor scooter with my hands under his butt. Someone had picked up my lifeless body, crumpled on the dance floor, called Anthony to come help get me home, and then put me on the bike behind him and only my hands under his butt were keeping me from falling off on the short ride home. When they put me in bed, they were smart enough to place a bucket on the floor near where my head was. I missed it the first time but had better aim as the night went on. The next day, while suffering from a monumental hangover, I went back to the disco and the bartender gave me my shirt.

ISRAEL

The weather started cooling enough that the Canadians and I decided Israel might be a good next destination. They talked about living on a kibbutz and how you could actually save a little money while living there and working, as well as have some fun. Many kibbutzim were even on the Mediterranean, adjacent to really nice beaches.

We flew over on an El Al 747 and were the only three passengers in coach. It was a pretty short flight and almost all the stewardesses were on a first name basis with us by the time we landed. They came over to where we were sitting and hung out with us virtually the whole flight. I really hit it off with one of them, an Italian named Patricia; so well, in fact, she had me come over to the Tel Aviv Hilton and spend the night with her. I had trouble with guards in the lobby of the hotel, walking in there with my long hair and a beard, but Patricia came down from her room to let the front desk staff know I was her guest.

The next day, I hooked up with my Canadian friends and went to a central office of the kibbutzim movement in Tel Aviv. Our first choice was any kibbutz on the Mediterranean but those were already full with no present openings for new volunteers. The Canadians chose a kibbutz called Sde Boker in the Negev Desert whose creation was inspired by the vision of the first prime minister of Israel, David Ben Gurion. It was to be where scientists and educators would work together in the Negev.

I chose another kibbutz, Yotvata, closer to the Red Sea. Its main source of revenue was a dairy as well as melons they exported to England. On the way down to start my life as a volunteer, I stopped for a few hours with my friends at Sde Boker. It was lunchtime and we got our trays of food and walked back to a table just across a small aisle from the table where Mr. Ben Gurion, by that time a very old man, was just finishing his lunch. I went over to him. "Mr. Gurion, my name is Ken Liss and I learned all about you from my mother and father. It's a real honor to meet you."

"Mr. Liss, the honor is mine. Thank you for saying hello." He was a sweet-looking old man.

Later, I bid my friends goodbye and got the late afternoon bus for the rest of the ride down south in the Negev Desert to Yotvata. It was in the large fields of melons there that I spent most of my work days. I would pick melons alongside the other three volunteers. Most kibbutzim had larger populations of members and had room for a good-sized number of volunteers who would usually live in barracks-type structures with many bunk beds around the room. At Yotvata, since it was so small, two volunteers shared a two-bedroom bungalow. There was a good-sized kitchen and bathroom there too. In front, there was a porch where I'd sit at lunch on warm days and get a few rays before heading back to the fields for yet more bins of melons.

The best meal each day was lunch when there'd be a huge amount of meat and vegetable choices during a pretty long lunch break. It allowed for a siesta before the final couple of hours of work for the day. The biggest part of the work day was morning. We'd be up very early, stop for some hot beverage and a couple of boiled eggs and bread, and right out to the fields we would go.

*****

The other volunteers on the kibbutz were a young lady from Sacramento, California, a guy from San Francisco, and my roommate, Scott, from San Diego. I was 24 at the time and Scott was a year younger. The four of us would walk behind the tractor and the three large bins it was carrying. We'd spread out in four adjacent rows, walking slowly and bending over to cut the ripe melons off their vines. Then we'd place them gently in the bins and continue this process until all the bins were filled. When that happened, the tractor would go back to the kibbutz's packing plants where they'd empty the bins and put the melons into crates ready for shipping to England where almost all of them would be sold.

While the tractor was returning to the packing plants, the four of us would sit down amidst the rows of melons, taking in the sun, eating a melon or two, and just tell stories. Howie, the guy from San Francisco, had just been in Ghana for a year or so. He was a real hustler. He'd worked from time to time as a freelance procurer of poisonous lizards, snakes, and insects that he would sell to zoos and aquariums around the world. In Ghana, he had tribes find the critters for him then smuggle them into Cameroon where he had a good relationship with the customs guys, aided by a little payola, who would allow for his shipments to be sent. He did this over and over again and had a passport with several extra pages that would fold out four-foot long with all the entry stamps from going back and forth. He had a million great stories and, over the course of the next couple of months, we heard many more than once.

One I really liked was when he went into Mexico for a day and found a dozen rattlesnakes that he put into his snake bag to bring back to Northern California for clients. At the border in Tijuana, the customs guy asked, "What's in that bag next to you?"

Howie told him, "I have a dozen rattlesnakes in it."

The agent said, "Follow me, sir, we're going into my office." Inside, he told Howie, "It is against the law to bring rattlesnakes to the USA from Mexico so you'll have to leave them."

Howie unzipped the bag and dumped them on the floor of the office. "This is my bag so here's the snakes!"

The agent jumped onto the top of his desk, pulled his gun out of his holster, and yelled to Howie, "OK, you can take the snakes. Get them out of here now!"

Another story I always enjoyed was of Howie's time in Ghana. Often in third world countries there was one version or another of American clubs. On regular occasions, the Westerners, not all from the States, would have dinner parties, dances, movie nights, etc. In Ghana at that time, Shirley Temple was the US ambassador. Howie had been to her house a few times for festive gatherings. There was a party one night and Howie had just come out of Shirley's house and, as he started up his vehicle, someone attacked him. The assailant jumped onto the running board of Howie's four-wheel drive and started grabbing at his face.

Howie returned the gesture, pushed back at his attacker's face, and then, with a big shove, pushed the guy away. He fell while Howie sped away. Howie then looked in his hand and realized, in the heat of the struggle, he had pulled the guy's ear off. He just tossed it out onto the road and drove home.

*****

The commitment of a volunteer on our kibbutz was working five and a half days a week. On Saturdays, we'd just work the morning and, if we wanted to travel to another part of the country, the kibbutz would give us bus fare to wherever we wanted to go. We had the afternoon and Sunday to enjoy somewhere but, when you went far, it was a bit of a tease because the majority of your time was on the bus. That's what happened the first weekend I took a trip and went from the kibbutz to Jerusalem. It took many hours, enough time to see Jerusalem in the late afternoon, sleep over, a morning of more sights, and then a long bus ride the rest of the day to get back by Sunday night. That pretty much shaped my decision-making on where to visit from that time on.

I loved the narrow streets in Jersualem's Old City with the little shops lining the street and people drinking milk tea and smoking hookahs. I was regularly followed by older men in the maze of alleys and constantly told by the Arabic guys how they were regularly harassed by the Jews. "We know you are a Jew," they said, "and we don't mean any harm to you or any others. We just want to live in peace." The Dome of the Rock, situated in the center of Temple Mount, was the first mosque I ever saw. Its enormous golden dome, glistening in the sun, was pretty impressive together with the daily calls to prayer. Along with the Wailing Wall, it's probably Jerusalem's most recognizable landmark.

When there were weekends I wanted to get away, I would just go down to Eilat, a tourist destination on the Red Sea at the southern tip of Israel, only an hour or so by bus. The first time I went, I hung out on a beach where lots of tourists were. Later in the day, I wandered toward the town and the beach near that area. This part was mostly populated by Israeli hippies. By the end of the night, when I put my sleeping bag down on the sand and passed out, I had already become part of the local scene and these guys were smoking and sharing some great hashish. Music was playing and it was certainly one element I missed while living the life of a volunteer on a kibbutz. The kibbutz was very straight.

I saw newspapers, old ones, copies of the *Jerusalem Post*, left around the entertainment center that were reminders to the kids there. These older editions had headlines like, "Local boy dies of marijuana overdose." Total baloney but effective propaganda.

Eilat, and specifically Coral Beach, was to be my new weekend destination. One of the beautiful things about hanging out there was watching the sunset and glancing over to see the city of Aqaba, across the sea in Jordan, lighting up. A spectacular sight to behold and one I saw on a number of occasions.

One Saturday on Coral Beach, I met a great English girl. We were in one of those restaurants where you dangle your toes in the sand. We kept eyeing each other. When she left, I saw her walk down on the beach to where she had her sleeping bag and backpack. It was very close to where my stuff was.

"Hey, how long have you been traveling?" A great ice breaker. "Want to smoke some hashish with me?"

"I thought you'd never ask," she said.

Well, one thing led to another and we ended up sleeping on the beach, cuddling the whole night. We had such a good time together I asked her, "How would you like to come back to my kibbutz with me tonight? You could stay in my bungalow without anyone knowing you're there and I could bring you food from the dining room."

"I wouldn't mind spending a few more days with you, Kenny."

We went back and I hid her in my bungalow for three days until the kibbutzniks figured out what was going on and made me tell her to leave. Up until that happened, she would eat the food I brought to her and we'd spend every free moment having sex and just holding on to one another. It was tough seeing her go.

*****

Howie was very much involved with the girl from Sacramento. They were always walking hand in hand and were visibly affectionate with one another; one happy couple. Scott and I were two young, horny guys. We had the good fortune to be living in a situation that was what maybe every young guy would dream of. Every young girl in Israel at that time was obligated to two years of service to the country after graduating high school.

The first few months after graduating, they would go through basic training in the Israeli Army. After the training was finished, they would spend the rest of their two years living on a kibbutz, being at the ready if necessary. So, during the last year of high school, a bus load of these girls would be sent to a kibbutz for a two-week orientation on kibbutz life. After two weeks, the girls who were already there would wait for the bus with the new girls who would get off and the others would get back on for their trip back home.

Scott and I would be there to see off the girls we'd been spending time with and to see, as they came down the steps of the bus, the ones we hoped to spend time with the next couple of weeks. It was the bus from bachelor heaven. Special delivery! Here they are, come and get 'em.

Scott would see one he liked and say, "Ken, she's mine. You get the next choice." And we'd switch back and forth with the first picks. Two I remember as really standing out were Mitza and Mazel, incredible-looking girls who were into knowing more about America and what I was all about.

My favorite though was a tall, athletic girl named Ruth. She wasn't as pretty as Mitza and Mazel but she was so much fun, so full of energy, and she could throw a mean frisbee. She and I just fell in love. At that time, I'd been on the kibbutz for about eight weeks. I was playing on the kibbutz basketball team and we had outdoor games under the lights. We'd travel around to different kibbutzim for road games and host a few home games too. I was the only foreigner on the team. Basketball was my game though.

I met a Swiss guy, Phillipe, who played for his kibbutz and, after the second time we played each other, we got talking.

"Ken, my family owns a hospital in Salisbury, Rhodesia. I'm flying to

Nairobi in a couple of weeks and then hitching down to Rhodesia to work in the hospital and make some money to continue my travels. If you come down there, I can get you a job there too if you're interested."

That was a nice offer but this was around the time Ruth and I were just getting to know and fall for each other. We dreaded the day her bus would come to take her away. Those two amazing weeks went by very fast. On Ruth's last night, I said to her, "Ruth, I'm crazy about you. I'd like to come see you in Tel Aviv. Would you like that?"

She didn't hesitate. "I'd love it if you came to see me. I'm crazy about you too and I think my parents would really like you."

"I want to move to your home town, Bat Yam, and eventually marry you."

"Ken, if you did live here and marry me, you'd have to go into the Israeli military."

"I don't care, Ruth. I did basic training in America and I'd do it again for you."

Before she got on the bus, she said, "Meet me at the main bus station in Tel Aviv next Saturday, under the big clock at exactly 5 p.m."

She might have told me more but I was never known for being a good listener. I was in such a state of rapture, I might have missed something. So eventually, I left my kibbutz. They were upset I wasn't staying longer. I took the long bus ride back to Tel Aviv and, all the way, I was on cloud nine, looking forward to starting a new life with this amazingly wonderful person.

I reached the bus station with plenty of time to spare. It was about 3:45 p.m. I quickly found the big clock and went to get something to eat across the street. I walked around the bus station just to kill time after eating and, to my horror, I saw a second big clock on the opposite side of the square-block station. *Two clocks! Which one will she be at?* At 4:55 p.m., I went to one of them, hoping she would be there and a little early. She wasn't there.

I walked calmly to the other end of the station and got there at 5 p.m. Not there either. I did a quick scan of people walking and tried to spot her. She wasn't there. I now ran back to the other side, hoping she would be there. It was 5:07 p.m. and she wasn't there.

I was sure I missed her at one of the clocks. I walked dejectedly away, not really knowing where I was going. Suddenly, on another side of the station, I realized there was a *third* big clock and I started beating myself up for not getting more information from her. What was her last name? I couldn't remember. She was just Ruth, the love of my life. The now forever-gone, love of my life.

I received a letter when I was at Yotvata from my cousin Bernie who was looking for me in Crete. He told me he was on a kibbutz studying Hebrew in the north of Israel. Now that I couldn't find Ruth, I figured I'd at least go visit Bernie. I took a bus up there to just outside of Haifa. His kibbutz had a huge orange farm and they did some type of manufacturing as well. He worked part of the time and studied Hebrew a portion of every day.

I found Bernie in the dining hall and we spent the evening catching up on his travels. There was an extra bed for me in the barracks where he lived. This kibbutz had many volunteers, somewhere around 50 of them. The next day, I asked Bernie if he'd like to go to East Africa with me. After failing to connect with Ruth, I remembered Phillipe telling me about Africa and I now wanted something new and different.

"No way will I consider Africa," Bernie replied. "I'm fine just being in Israel."

I went and bought a dirt-cheap plane ticket to Nairobi, Kenya, using my international student card. They had amazingly great deals for young students back in those days. Bernie asked the kibbutz if he could take a couple of days off and go to Tel Aviv with me.

When we reached Tel Aviv, we changed our clothes. Bernie had with him two really cool warm-up uniforms that athletes from the Olympic village gave him when he was in Munich for the '72 games and we changed into them. In August that year, he'd flown to Reykjavik, Iceland, for the Boris Spassky vs. Bobby Fischer chess matches. He would call me at my job in San Francisco at night using a fake account to give me updates. While there, he ran into a guy he knew from San Francisco who worked for KGO TV, an ABC affiliate, who was phoning reports back to the station for nightly updates of the match. He told Bernie to look him up in Munich.

When he went there, the same guy was able to get Bernie an ABC blazer for a couple of days. Bernie wore it to the Olympic village and got an interview with the coach of the USA track team. Bernie was great at acting like a reporter. At the end of the interview, he asked the coach if he could borrow one of the USA warm-up uniforms for some promotion shots. He'd bring it back in 24 hours. He took the ABC TV blazer back to his acquaintance from San Francisco and, now he had a USA uniform, he could come and go as he pleased in the Olympic village. He ended up staying with the Puerto Rico basketball team players whose rooms were right across from the rooms of the Israeli team.

So, in his bag in that room in Tel Aviv, he had a Puerto Rico warm-up and a USA warm-up. I wore the USA uniform and Bernie the Puerto Rican one to the office of the Israeli Olympic committee. We told them we were in Munich when the tragedy happened and wanted to pay our respects to the athletes who were murdered. They had a rep take us to one of the cemeteries where a few of the fallen team members were buried and then he took us out to lunch. It was a sad afternoon to be sure.

We decided to do a quick trip to Jerusalem since my flight to Nairobi was a couple of days away. We got on a *sherut*, a half-sized bus, and headed east. About an hour or so into the ride, our bus driver got into a road rage scene with a truck driver heading in the same direction. The truck would pass us and our driver would swear out loud then he'd time it and pass the truck. This went back and forth and the drivers made wild gestures at one another.

About twenty minutes into this battle, our driver passed the truck and then, once in front of it, he slowed and slowed then jammed on his brakes. The truck hit us from behind. Our driver opened the door, got out, and began yelling at the truck driver for rear-ending us but, honestly, it was our driver's fault. People on the *sherut* had been yelling at our driver to mellow out the whole time and he wouldn't listen. Now, we sat in the bus for an hour until police came. Several of the Israeli passengers got out and spoke to the police, obviously giving their interpretation of what happened. The police arrested our driver along with the truck driver and we had to wait another couple of hours for the next *sherut* to come pick us up. Road rage knows no geographical bounds.

The next day went by quickly. Another Jerusalem wham bam, in and out, and we were back in Tel Aviv getting ready for my flight to Nairobi and Bernie's return to his kibbutz.

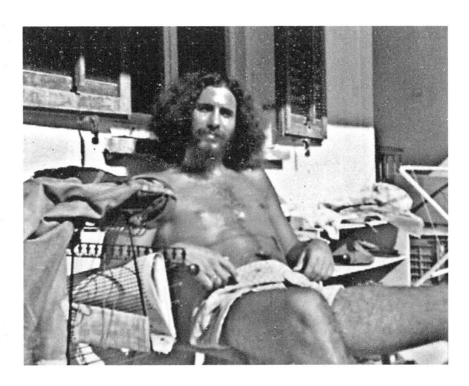

In front of my bungalow.

KENYA

I flew to Nairobi and was seated on the flight next to Richard Yala, a native of the Lake Victoria area in Kenya. He was very outgoing so the long flight was much easier to deal with, listening to all his stories about Kenya, told in his impeccable Queen's English.

Richard said, "Ken, I have a nice home on the shores of the lake and I'd be very honored if you would come to see my home town, Homa Bay, and be my house guest for a while. I think you'll really like my family as well." I was pretty excited to have made a Kenyan friend before having even arrived in the country and looked forward to seeing Lake Victoria, the second largest freshwater lake in the world behind Lake Superior.

We arrived in Nairobi pretty late in the evening so he suggested we get a hotel room to share and, after another day in the capital city, we'd then set off to his home town.

We found a pretty cheap hotel and, as soon as we got settled in, Richard called room service and asked if they had a woman who might be able to come up and join us for the night. When he hung up he said, "Ken, you'll really like the ladies here in Kenya."

"Richard, I'm exhausted from all that flying so whoever the room service sends up here to the room is all yours, my friend. I promise to keep my eyes closed and not watch as you two fool around."

There was a knock on the door and in walked the lady. While Richard was closing the door behind her, she asked where she should put her clothes and then she immediately said to Richard, "Who's your little friend, hiding under the blanket?" She pulled the blanket off me and I was so startled I opened my eyes and will never be able to get that image out of my mind. She was a giant of a woman.

She said to me, "Son, you might want to join us." I thanked her for her offer, begged off as politely as I could, and then pulled the blanket over my head again. She and Richard sounded like they had a grand old time and, to my surprise, when I woke up the following morning, his bed was still standing, in one piece. I didn't think any structure would be able to withstand that much abuse.

When we went outside that morning, there were major goings-on all around the city. It turned out it was the ninth anniversary of Kenya's independence from England. Buses drove by with people hanging out of every window and lying on their rooftops, heading to a stadium outside of town where the celebration was happening. Richard and I got on a bus, totally engulfed by locals, and stood for the whole twenty-minute ride. We got off at a large park near the stadium where there were many tribes in full costume practicing their dances and waiting for their turn to march into the stadium to eventually rotate around until they performed in front of the review stand where Jomo Kenyatta, the first president of Kenya, sat. He was sitting there, swatting flies with his famous giraffe hair flyswatter.

After a particular tribe had performed for a couple of minutes, all the tribes circling the stadium in full regalia would rotate and, one by one, leave the stadium as others replaced them. There was a constant beat of drums that went on for hours. It was a great time and, when we finally tired of the scene, we headed back into town and Richard visited with some cousins in projects that were pretty depressing. I'm not sure what he was doing, possibly there to help them out with a few shillings.

Later, in the early evening while I was walking around near the hotel, I ran into Phillipe, the Swiss guy I met playing basketball in Israel. "Hey, Phillipe, what a small world. I didn't think I would find you here."

"Ken, I didn't expect you were going to come down here at all. A great surprise, my friend. This is Steve and this is Brad and we're all going to travel down to Moshi in Tanzania and climb Mount Kilimanjaro. Are you up for that? We'll meet a week from today at the Moshi YMCA in Tanzania."

That sounded like a great plan to me. Phillipe and Steve would hitch together and I would hitch with Brad. I was looking forward to some fun times on the way to Moshi.

"Ken, let's meet for breakfast tomorrow and talk a little more about the plan."

I told Richard later that I was going to pass on going with him to Homa Bay. He was disappointed to be sure.

The next morning, I met Phillipe and Brad, a mountain climbing instructor from Utah, and Steve, a school teacher from Portland, Oregon. After breakfast, we hit the road. The first thing Brad and I did was to hitch a ride from a guy with a large stake truck. In the back were several Maasai warriors, standing around with spears and shields. We stood with them as we headed down a long road.

After several hours over bumpy roads, a long distance and way out in the bush, flat and seemingly never-ending in any direction, one of the Maasai knocked on the top of the cab and the driver slowed down and stopped. It was the strangest thing to me as I looked in the direction the warrior started running. There was no landmark in the distance to indicate a town or village but run he did and he kept running until we drove down the road far enough to see he'd disappeared into the distance. I often wondered what it was he saw on that long road that triggered that he knew he was at the right place to get off the truck.

After another long stretch of about five hours, we came to a town called Narok. We still had a long way to go and, luckily, we ran into a game park ranger who was loading his Land Rover with supplies. We started up a conversation and found he was heading further along the road toward Maasai Mara. He offered us a ride for as far as he was going which was to a small village with grass and mud huts, just off a main road. When we arrived, he spoke in Swahili to a young man who then turned to us and spoke very good English. While the park ranger was busy unloading some supplies for them, almost all the villagers crowded around us and became engrossed in a loud shouting match. As quickly as it started, they stopped.

The young man, Peter, turned to us. "The families here feel it would be an honor for you guys to sleep in their hut tonight. Whoever gets the honor will sleep outside or find someone else who wants to let them sleep in their hut, even if it is very cramped."

We tried to protest, feeling like we were putting a family out of their own place, but they wouldn't hear of it. It was an honor for them to let us stay in their home and they weren't asking how we felt anyway. They were all fighting for that honor. So, we took our packs to the hut of the family who eventually won the discussion, placed them inside, and then Peter took us around to each and every hut in the circular village so each family could offer us something to show us their hospitality.

The huts were made of mud and thatch mixed together. Their floors were hardened mud and there were tanned goat hides placed around on the floor for sleeping on, one for each family member. There were also at least one or two small, crude wooden stools. Most of the people offered us a milky-looking beverage that was somewhat fermented. The hygiene was questionable but there was no way we would turn down anything offered to us.

"Hey, Peter, is there a place where me and Brad could get something to eat in this village?" I asked eventually.

He took us to a double-sized hut that had a few tables and an adjoining kitchen. "We have a meat and vegetable stew today," he said. He brought us each a big plate along with a few slices of bread to scoop up the gravy. It was pretty darn good. When we were done, he told us it would cost us the equivalent of around 25 cents. We played around with him, telling him, "Hey, we're not rich people; that's a lot of money. Can we get some dessert with the meal for that price?"

"We don't have anything else." He shrugged.

"Is it OK if we take a look in the kitchen?"

He pointed the way and followed us in. We saw a pretty neat-looking area with shelves filled with gallon cans of milk, butter, and plum jam as well as rows of fresh-looking loaves of bread. We asked if they had eggs and he pulled out a flat with eggs too. There was a round, twelve-inch thick slab of steel that was maybe 30 inches in diameter and it was just above a large container of red-hot wood embers.

"Is it OK if we use some of the ingredients in the kitchen to make a dessert?" I asked. He told us to go right ahead. Brad and I knew exactly what we were going to make. We found an already-open container of milk and whipped an egg into it. We sliced some bread into nice thick slices, dipped it into the milk/egg mixture, and plopped it onto the slab of hot steel. Peter then brought us some butter and jam and we slathered it onto the cooked bread and told him to try our French toast. He had two bites and then called the cook to come join us. They both loved it.

The next morning, Peter woke us. "Come outside and see what's going on," he said. There was a line of the villagers waiting for us at the restaurant hut. Peter said, "They all want to try the French toast," so Brad and I spent the next couple of hours making it for everyone. After we were done, we told them we wanted to continue our journey so Peter and his younger brother helped us carry our packs out to the main road where we could try getting a ride. We sat on the side of the road, waiting for cars to pass. There weren't many as this wasn't exactly an area with any real traffic.

We sat with some of the guys from the village who didn't seem to have anything better to do than watch us play with a frisbee. They had some joints they lit up and shared with us. These guys had a bow and some crude arrows and we let them try and shoot the frisbee and, on a couple of occasions, they actually hit it and knocked it off course. Luckily the arrows had no sharp metal tips so the frisbee wasn't damaged. We had a jolly good time getting high with them.

A couple of their women passed by carrying large gourds, put them down, and proceeded to throw the frisbee with us. They actually threw it better than the guys did, maybe because they weren't stoned. This was also a good opportunity with all the free time we had for me to pull out my copy of *Atlas Shrugged*, Ayn Rand's magnum work of fiction depicting a dystopian US, which I was really wanting to finish so I could lighten my load. It was such a big book yet impossible to leave behind without finishing.

*****

We ended up getting a ride to Keekorok Lodge from a couple who were going to be staying there for a few days. It was the first lodge built in the Maasai Mara and was erected in the direct path of the wildebeest migration. The rooms were way too expensive for Brad and me. Behind the resort there was a row of hut-like offices. One of them was the office of the resident game warden who worked for the lodge. We asked him if he was OK if we slept on his floor and he agreed it was fine since he wasn't there at night.

It took us two days to get a ride from Keekorok Lodge to the border with Tanzania. In the mornings, we'd sit on the road outside the lodge, trying to flag down someone heading to the border and ultimately into Serengeti. In the afternoons, we were able to swim in the pool at the lodge. From the bungalows and pool area, there was a large amount of land visible where all kinds of wildlife crossed in front of the guests. What a comfortable way to view the big game of Africa, from a chaise longue at the pool. It was another good place for me to read my book, too. Enough already with *Atlas Shrugged*'s John Galt and Francisco.

Brad and I ate at the small bar restaurant behind the lodge for the employees to hang out in when their shifts were over. On its porch, there was a Coleman lantern hanging about head high with a zillion flying bugs of all sizes swirling around it. We had to pass through that swarm to get inside and just going into that place was a big mistake for me. I had long frizzy hair and a frizzy beard. Those flying critters got all tangled up in my hair and beard and drove me crazy for the whole night. The next morning, I shaved my beard before we started looking for a ride. Enough was enough.

Richard and me.

Phillipe, on left, and Richard.

Tribes from all over Kenya performed in the park before they went into the stadium.

Tribes from all over Kenya performed in the park before they went into the stadium.

Tribes from all over Kenya performed in the park before they went into the stadium.

Tribes from all over Kenya performed in the park before they went into the stadium.

Peter with my pack. His brother with Brad's pack.

The lady put her gourds down and tossed the frisbee with us. She was very good.

The offices at Keekorok Lodge. It was raining and then the rainbows appeared.

TANZANIA

After almost two days of trying to get a ride, the lodge's game warden was kind enough to take us to the border where we got out and tried our hand at hitching again. Two border guards there looked at people's passports as they passed through. That night, after not being able to get a ride, the guards offered their hut to us to sleep in and cooked up some maize and shared that with us too. We ended up staying with them for two nights, eating maize with them a couple of times the following day. It was pretty much like eating over-cooked cream of wheat, a solid slab of wet, tasteless, hot cereal.

It was hot as hell there. At night, it was impossible to lie in the sleeping bag so I'd lie on top of it. Those hard-packed mud floors were no better than the cement floors in the game warden's office at the lodge so the bag offered little padding. The difference though was that the warden's office had walls that were covered by the roof. The border guards' hut had a space of six inches or so between the top of the wall and the thatch roof, which allowed any mosquitos in the neighborhood to fly inside and get us. It was tough sleeping with them swarming around. My feet and arms suffered the most.

During the daytime, we took a hike around the hills and stream nearby with one of the guards. As we passed a particular tree, he pointed. "There are lions over there. You should look them in the eyes as you pass by. Otherwise, if you look away, they'll attack you." We walked right by that tree, looking at the animals in a state of total fear. It worked though. None of them even moved. The whole time, I was humming the song "The Lion Sleeps Tonight" to myself. *A-weema-weh, a-weema-weh, a-weema-weh, a-weema-weh.*

The amount of energy we felt walking around out there was off the charts. It was as if we'd consumed many cups of coffee. On the morning of the third day, a Combi, which was the term they used when talking about a VW van, stopped at the border. It was a Dutch couple from Nairobi on their way to Seronera Wildlife Lodge in the heart of Serengeti. We told them we were headed that way and the guy suggested, "I can take you guys all the way there but I only have room for one inside the van so one of you'll have to sit on the roof, on the luggage rack." Brad and I decided to take turns up there. We bid the guards goodbye and thanked them for their hospitality and took off, with me on top.

About twenty minutes into the ride, the van slowed and I could hear the sound of a movie camera filming. Alongside us, a rhino appeared, running slowly. I immediately got a little nervous and began pounding with my feet on the rack to let the guy know I'd like to get moving. Finally, the driver sped the van up and we lost the rhino. Another twenty minutes or so went by and the van totally stopped. On a hillside off to our left was a big bull elephant. The camera started filming again. I could hear its motor.

The elephant slowly came down the hill and was now just a few feet from the van. It's a good thing I'd taken a dump that morning because I was really so scared I would have shit in my pants. The tusks on that elephant were huge and I remembered hearing stories about rogue elephants sometimes turning cars over and just stomping around on them. I started knocking repeatedly on the roof of that Combi, trying to let them know of my terror. Finally, they got the hint and took off, quickly putting some distance between us and the elephant.

After we were safely away from it, the driver stopped and Brad and I changed places. We then continued our ride for miles and miles through Serengeti, seeing amazing large herds of wildebeest, zebras, gazelles of all types, and even watched a couple of cheetahs make a kill. It was a scene I've watched many times since on wildlife specials but this time it was in person.

We passed by a spot where another kill had taken place earlier. The big cats were gone and now there was a carcass with a mountain of vultures climbing all over each other while picking at the leftover meat on the bones. Hovering around the birds were a couple of hyenas waiting for their turn. The ugliness of those birds was actually surpassed by the hyenas. They really are nasty-looking animals.

*****

Finally, we made it to Seronera Lodge where Brad and I sat down at an outdoor café and had a big meal. While there, we met some Aussies who'd been on a trip for several months that started in London and continued down into West Africa, across central Africa and the Congo, and they were now on the last leg of their trip in East Africa. They were traveling in one of those old army Deuce-and-a-Half trucks with the rollup canvas sides.

"Hey, guys, where are you headed?" I asked.

"We're on our way to Ngorongoro Crater in Tanzania."

"Brad and I are going to Moshi but Ngorongoro's on the way. Could we hitch a ride?"

"Sure, we can take you and even have a tent for you but it doesn't have a fly."

It sounded good to us so, after eating, we got into the truck with about ten others and drove outside the grounds of the lodge to an area they said was where we'd set up camp for the night. Brad and I put up the tent they gave us and they apologized again and again that there was no fly for it. The fly was a sheet of canvas that goes above the tent to deflect any rain that might occur during the night. We didn't care. It was a beautiful night and we were just happy to have a ride. The tent was icing on the cake.

Finally, we all turned in. We discovered another small glitch with the tent — the zipper to close it was broken. *No big deal*, we thought. It didn't take too long to realize the open tent was an invitation for mosquitos to come inside. I was still having a problem with the bites from the previous nights at the border and didn't want to add to it. So, I got inside the sleeping bag but still those buggers buzzed my ears non-stop.

I put my whole head inside the bag and just let my nose stick out so I could breathe some relatively cool air. It was incredibly hot inside the bag. All of a sudden, I heard a crack of thunder and, shortly after that, a downpour of rain. It started hitting the tent really hard and, with no fly, the water came right through and collected on the bottom of the tent, the one part that was waterproof. The water came in fast and, within fifteen minutes, it was probably two to three inches deep and my bag was soaked, inside and out. This was very uncomfortable being totally drenched and sweating inside my bag trying to shield myself from the mosquitos.

Suddenly, to make matters worse, much worse, something large outside the tent decided to lie down against the side, right up against our heads.

"Brad, what's that?" I muttered.

"I don't know, Ken, but be very still."

Whatever it was, you could feel its musculature and hear that it was chewing on something. My heart started pounding like crazy. My imagination was running wild. What was lying against us outside the tent? I was hyperventilating. Brad kept whispering to me, "Ken, be still. Be quiet, please," but I couldn't control my heavy breathing. I was scared out of my mind.

We noticed that the sounds of it eating stopped for a while. In an instant, we found out exactly what it was that was out there, lying against us. There was a loud roar. Holy shit, it was a lion.

Brad got up and started trying to fix the zipper on the tent. It didn't work. He reached into his pack and found three safety pins and closed the flaps with them. I just lay there, praying to have a heart attack and get off

57

easily. This was not how I wanted to go out of the world, eaten by a hungry lion.

We lay there all wet, with mosquitos having a field day on us and that lion pressed up against our heads. There was nowhere to go. After what seemed like an eternity, the pressure against the tent was gone and obviously so was the lion. The next thing I knew, it was morning. We had finally drifted off and slept.

Oh, happy day, was all that came to mind when I saw the sun had started coming up. The Rascals' song "It's a Beautiful Morning" swirled around my head. When we got out of the tent, we found a large bone next to it. We asked the other people if the lion had woken them up. Nobody had heard it. The rain against the tent was loud so I guess it was feasible they didn't hear the lion roar. They were all dry in their tents with no mosquitos getting in and they'd slept right through our hours of terror. But we did at least have a bone to back up our story.

*****

That day, we began our drive to Ngorongoro Crater, the largest intact caldera in the world. It has an area of about 100 square miles and is home to the big five of African wildlife — rhino, elephants, lions (the black mane ones), leopards, and Cape buffalo — among other species. After the rain of the night before, the roads were really wet and muddy. We were cruising along at roughly 25 miles an hour over muddy roads when, all of a sudden, we couldn't move. We were stuck in mud.

"OK, everyone out of the truck," said the driver. They had a one-foot-wide and six-foot-long metal slab they put under the back wheels that were stuck. We all stood behind the truck and pushed as hard as we could while the driver tried to get the wheels to grab onto something and move out of the mud. With all the mosquito bites I had on my feet and lower legs, being knee deep in mud was just wonderful, except for the fact that, just a few feet away, walking parallel to us, was a congress of baboons. Some of them had babies hanging upside down from their mother's stomach. To see them up close was pretty unsettling. The adults had huge teeth, very sharp looking too. They finally passed us by but no sooner had they done so than we saw, lurking up in a nearby tree, a sleeping leopard, both its front and back legs straddling a thick branch.

I suddenly realized how vulnerable we all were out there and how little we could do about the animals except just ignore them if we possibly could. Finally, with one big push after almost 30 minutes of trying, we extricated ourselves from the mud. On to Ngorongoro Crater. We got there too late in the day to go into the actual crater so we set up camp on the edge near a lodge and bought some take-out from their restaurant. It was the first time I'd eaten a meat dish with plantains. I didn't much care for them but we were very hungry and they did fill you up.

Having finished setting up our tent, I walked around not far from our camping area. I heard some heavy thrashing in the trees and stopped and waited. Then I saw an elephant. I was lucky I had my little instamatic camera. I took a shot but the elephant looked too small in the frame so I walked closer and closer to try and get a better shot. I was really jealous of all the Aussies on that truck as they all had SLRs with big zoom lenses.

I took another couple of shots of the elephant and, all of a sudden, it took a few running steps toward me with foliage being crushed as it got nearer. I didn't wait. I took off, running toward camp, and was relieved it didn't continue chasing me. I realized how dangerous it can be when you're in the natural habitat of these amazing animals though.

Next day, we got permission to drive down into the crater with the truck. The crater had a big lake in it and, from the top, it looked pink. When we got down inside, that pink turned out to be thousands of flamingos. We drove to another part of the crater which was very anti-climactic since it wasn't full of wildlife and anything you saw, like the black-maned lion, had a dozen Land Rovers surrounding it. It was impossible to take a photo of the lion without a Land Rover in the background. A real disappointment as far as the ratio of wildlife to tourists.

*****

That was the end of our travels with the Aussies who were headed for Lake Manyara game reserve but we met a guy with room in his Combi that could take us as far as Arusha. Brad and I needed to get moving if we were going to meet our friends in Moshi for the Kilimanjaro climb. On the way toward Arusha, the owner of the Combi, another Dutch guy, saw a village in the distance, not far from the side of the road we were driving on. He pulled off. It was a Maasai village. There were a number of young warriors there and we parked and got out. The Dutch guy asked if he could take their picture and they agreed if he gave them some money, which he did. Then he took a few shots and something freaked them out. They started running toward us and we quickly jumped in the Combi and started driving away. We weren't fast enough to avoid having two of the tires popped by their spears and the rear window broken. The Combi just limped down the road for the next 45 minutes, all the way to Arusha.

Arusha is mainly famous for being the gateway city to some of the best landscapes and game parks in Africa. It's also the place where you could

59

find high quality products made of meerschaum, mainly smoking pipes. The first thing the driver did was stop at the police station to file a complaint about the Maasai who'd attacked his Combi. The police chief interviewed him and told him he would have to go with him back to the village and point out who was responsible. Not surprisingly, he didn't want to go back there and see them face to face so the police chief told him to forget about filing any charges and showed him where the closest auto repair shop was.

It was late in the day and there was a park right behind the police station so Brad and I decided to sleep out under the stars. We took turns going to get some food while the other one watched our packs. After getting comfy in our sleeping bags, someone came over to us.

"Hey, guys, you shouldn't sleep in the park." It was a policeman from the station. "It's way too dangerous. There are too many criminals hanging around the park."

"Know anywhere we can go instead?" I asked him.

"You'll be much safer if you come inside the station." I didn't expect that offer. He pointed to a hallway. "You can sleep in here but, as soon as it's light, you'd better leave."

What a great guy. The next morning, we left for Moshi, now only a short journey away, and we finally arrived at the YMCA where we'd planned to meet up with Phillipe and Steve. It also had the bonus of a nice pool with a gorgeous, unobstructed view of the mountain. What a great starting point for what would hopefully be an amazing climb.

The Aussies were on the road for months before they took Brad and me on board.

The elephant I saw at Ngorongoro Crater.

The border guards enjoyed playing frisbee with us.

KILIMANJARO

Brad and I had made it to the YMCA just in time for the Kilimanjaro trip. Not only was there Steve, Phillipe, Brad, and me but also Daniel, a guy who'd met up with Phillipe and Steve before Brad and I arrived. Daniel, an English guy, was a first mate on cargo ships and had just ridden his BMW bike up from Durban. He looked just like the guy on the cover of Zig-Zag rolling-paper packs. We sat down at the pool and got to know each other.

I remembered Steve had a cassette of *Thick as a Brick*, Jethro Tull's latest album. We partied for a couple of days, listening often to that cassette, and then started talking seriously about the climb, even going to the library in Moshi to check out the different routes up the mountain. We didn't want to do the YMCA trip. First of all, it cost people a hundred dollars or so to go that way and, second, it was a couple of days more on the mountain. We wanted to get up and down as quickly as possible and do it for free.

Brad found the Mweka route and its starting point. We could take a bus there with our supplies and head up through forest the first day. We decided on what we needed for supplies and went to a store to buy everything. Daniel had a small propane stove so we bought a couple of packages of Knorr soup then added in a bunch of cans of corned beef, fresh fruit, some loaves of bread, candy bars, cookies, and two five-gallon plastic canisters to carry water in. We then had a big meal the night before we set out.

Early the next morning, we took a bus to Moshi and then another to our starting point which was at 5,600 ft. We hiked for a couple of hours to a clearing and had breakfast before setting out into a beautiful forest with a narrow path to follow up and up and up. There were numerous switchbacks and, after a while, each tree looked the same with a ton of moss hanging from the trunks and branches. Birds sang and chirped as we huffed and puffed upwards, looking for any diversion to take our minds off the physical strain.

Many times, we saw gorgeous, wildly colored mushrooms, sometimes five or six inches across. We hiked for a good five hours after the breakfast break and finally came out to a clearing. We'd passed the forest and now there was fairly sparse vegetation. We were at around 10,000 ft and there was the first night's accommodation, a corrugated metal circular hut, maybe 12 ft. in diameter. It had a door so we could protect ourselves from any wind. We sat down, got comfy, passed a couple of joints around, and ate some food. Shortly after eating, our teacher from Seattle, Steve, complained of dizziness and nausea. He was up all night, going outside with a very bad case of the shits and vomiting. He didn't get any sleep at all. The rest of us slept like babies.

We woke up at the break of day. It was sunny and clear. Steve told us there was no way he could continue on. He was sick as a dog and to go any further he'd be a burden for sure. He said he would go down on his own and see us back at the YMCA. It was a disappointing start to our climb.

*****

Already we were down to four team members. We took off for the next day's ascent, taking turns carrying the water canisters. Man, oh man, water is heavy. We switched quite often. The first interesting thing we noticed was how, at that altitude, there was very little in the way of signs of life and then eventually there was nothing. On rocks along the way, we saw lichens early in the day and then less and less of them. There were no birds up in the high altitude either.

When the sun shone, it was very warm while we were exerting ourselves. As soon as clouds came between us and the sun, the temperature dropped dramatically. During the walk, we were able to handle the temperature fluctuations since our body temperatures were pretty high from our exertion.

The mountain wasn't all up a steep incline. There were vast fields we crossed, always looking for the three rocks piled up, which was the marking that indicated we were on the proper trail. Some of those vast fields had no real path and we walked across many football-field lengths on what seemed like chunks of broken dishes. They weren't very stable under foot either and we had to be careful not to slip and fall on them. The altitude made breathing more difficult than the day before but we'd stop and rest every few hundred yards and gladly drink some of our water to continually lighten that load.

It was a long day and we finished up at 4:30 p.m. at the second and last hut at around 16,000 ft. There was nothing but clouds around us and it gave me a feeling of claustrophobia. The visibility was very poor and I had a pounding headache. Daniel rolled a couple of joints and lit one up. I didn't want anything to do with getting high at this point. I was already feeling very weak. My body was aching and Daniel forced me to drink a bunch of water and then made some Knorr chicken noodle soup and wouldn't leave me alone until I had a good portion.

The pain in my head was relentless. I snuggled up in my sleeping bag which was a good down bag and supposedly good to twenty below zero. I lay in it and shivered all night long. I don't think I slept for more than an hour. The cold and the pounding headache gave me hard-core chills.

At 5 a.m., the sun started coming up and there was major activity in the hut. Daniel and Brad convinced us to take some plastic bags we had and put them around our socks and then put on our boots. Phillipe had no boots at all, just some Birkenstocks. He put on a couple of pairs of socks and the plastic bags around his feet. We decided not to carry the water canisters. Not for this final ascent where we would need every ounce of strength just to get ourselves up the mountain's steepest part. This route we took, the Mweka, was one of the steepest routes but also the shortest too. It was pretty difficult but we wouldn't have to spend all that time like some of the other routes that take six or seven days up.

We knew we'd be walking on volcanic ash and between tall glacier walls so, if we needed water, we'd just break icicles off the glacier and suck on them like popsicles. We ate well before we left. My headache was gone.

The day was picture perfect, sunny and clear. We could see Mount Meru in the distance and I started humming some loud and fast music as we set out for the last day's climb. "Dazed and Confused," a Led Zeppelin song, played over and over in my head. It didn't take long to realize how difficult this final day was going to be.

Daniel and I went straight up on the ash. Brad and Phillipe went off to the side to walk on the glacier. We told them we'd meet them back at the first day's hut if we didn't see them at the top. Daniel was in great shape and provided me a with lot of inspiration, talking to me about everything under the sun and not complaining about the lack of oxygen.

By the time we were above 17,000 ft., it became very slow going. We walked just a few yards away from the glacier wall. It must have been fifteen to twenty feet high and there were tons of icicles, many way too thick to break off for some cool relief. We found enough of the smaller sized ones though to satisfy our thirst.

By noon, we were up around 18,000 ft. and it was very difficult to sustain more than a few steps' momentum at a time without taking a rest. The biggest problem was that the ash was softer than sand and, each step you'd take, you'd slide back two thirds of the way. It made the climb much more difficult.

I finally got to the point after another hour where I was on my hands and knees, crawling up. I could make it a few feet upwards and then I'd have to rest a couple of minutes. Daniel kept egging me on. By 2 p.m., we were up around the 19,000 ft. mark. I was getting very sick. My body was aching. My joints were on fire and I felt feverish. I sat and looked out at the view and I couldn't move.

Daniel came over and shook me. "Ken, are you OK, brother?"

I don't even remember responding. I just sat there, staring off into space. He took off for the summit. I'm not sure how much time passed but, all of a sudden, he grabbed my arm and stood me up. He said he'd made the summit and we now needed to start down. I just wanted to curl up and go to sleep, right there. I didn't care about anything at that point.

Daniel held onto me and started sliding downwards. The gravity made me take some long steps and then he jumped up in the air and I followed him. It was like flying. I ran a couple more steps down and launched myself into the air and I must have flown ten feet and then, when my feet hit the ash, I slid down and fought to keep my balance. I was feeling a rush of adrenalin and life in my body and mind all of a sudden. This was fun!

We continued to take some quick steps and fly down the mountain for the next fifteen or twenty minutes. The further down we went, the more I felt like myself again. The fever was disappearing and my body didn't hurt as much. Going down was what the doctor ordered. Who woulda thunk it? Up there, I wasn't thinking at all. My mind was on total shutdown.

Now, we were almost at the hut. When we got there and went in, one of the water canisters was gone and Brad's and Phillipe's packs were gone too. We knew we'd have to meet them at the hut down at 10,000 ft. We got our stuff and started off. After going way down, I noticed that where the sun was in the sky was different than the day before. We stopped and took stock of the situation and realized we were going down the wrong way. We had to traverse the mountain for a good hour to find the right trail before heading down the rest of the way. We barely made it to the hut before it got dark. That might have been a whole different adventure if we didn't make it before total darkness enveloped us.

While going down, I noticed a burning sensation on my right foot. I had no problem with my feet on the way up the mountain but, all of a sudden, each step the last couple of hours going down I felt something very noticeably wrong. I noticed my foot sliding forward inside my boot. The boots weren't actually mine. On the kibbutz in Israel, I used boots I found in their equipment room where they also had lots of clothing the volunteers could wear while working in the fields so as not to ruin their own. The boots weren't a perfect fit but walking on flat ground never really put me to the test.

When we got into the hut, Brad and Phillipe immediately opened a bottle of champagne to celebrate. Daniel had bought it when we got our food supplies, knowing it would be Christmas Eve when we got back to the lower hut and we'd be in the mood for a party. We smoked some joints, sipped champagne, and laughed about our difficulties going for the summit. It turned out Brad and Phillipe gave up earlier also, having felt pretty sick from the altitude. Phillipe had had a difficult time walking up the glacier with the Birkenstocks.

While the guys were partying, I decided to take off my boot and see what was causing the pain. When I peeled the sock off, the right side of my heel had a blood blister almost two inches long. After a few minutes of deliberation, I borrowed a safety pin from Brad and popped and drained the blister. I was hoping against all reason that it might feel good the next morning when we were to go down.

I woke up at the crack of dawn, got dressed, and put my boots back on. Just a couple of steps inside the hut and I knew I was in trouble. I saw Daniel. "Dan, I'm gonna start down before the rest of you guys. Maybe I can get far enough down that we can all get down to the bottom at the same time." I hobbled down, with every step being very difficult. After a couple of hours, I heard the three guys coming up on me already. We had a few laughs, wished each other a Merry Christmas, and then they disappeared and my plan of all of us reaching the bottom together dissolved.

When I finally made it down, I was at a farm and I tried to recall where we'd got off the bus just a few days before. I finally remembered it was a good quarter of a mile from where I was but I was really spent and couldn't even imagine walking 50 ft. I sat down and, after a half hour, a pickup truck came my way. I flagged it down and the driver stopped. I asked him if he could give me a ride to the YMCA and he said he'd do it for $20. That worked for me.

That night, Dan, Brad, Phillipe, and I headed to Moshi and had dinner in a restaurant that was very much into the Christmas spirit. We all got drunk and stuffed with a great hot meal. The next day, after some major pool time which was welcome after the previous days' trekking, we went into the YMCA café. While we were sitting in our booth, an American guy and his wife asked us if we had climbed Kilimanjaro. We told him we'd just got down the day before. He asked if he could take a few pictures with us and sat in our booth while his wife took the pictures. I guess, to him, we were some kind of celebrities.

Mount Kilimanjaro from YMCA pool.

First morning on Kilimanjaro. Steve, the guy in the dark shirt and jeans, is the one who got sick the first night and went back down.

With our stomachs full, we're ready to push on to the first night's hut.

Just leaving the first night's hut for our second day's ascent on
Kilimanjaro.

Early morning, third day, from the hut.

After setting out on the third morning, I noticed Mount Meru in background.

MOSHI TO MOMBASA

That afternoon, I started feeling pretty lousy. Phillipe told me he was trying to score a ride for the two of us so we could move on toward Zimbabwe and the jobs waiting for us at the hospital. I decided to get a room at the YMCA because I felt like shit and had a fever coming on. Sleeping outside just didn't cut it, the way I was feeling.

The next morning, Phillipe came into the room. "Ken, I found a ride all the way to Zambia, which is very close to Rhodesia and where jobs are waiting for us."

"I feel like shit, Phillipe. I think you'll have to go on your own. I appreciate you considering me for a job there."

He said he'd try to stall the driver but, if I wasn't out there in a couple of hours, he'd have to go. I didn't make it. Phillipe left and I had to stay one more night to try and recover. I didn't like spending the money that room was costing me but it made a difference sleeping with some comfort.

I woke up the following day feeling much better and, although I felt bad I missed the chance to go with Phillipe, I did still have Daniel and Brad to bounce new ideas with for destinations. After hanging at the pool all day, Daniel informed me we needed to go into Moshi and find something to smoke. He'd run out. Brad wasn't into it so he stayed behind.

Daniel and I walked down the street that night and asked a couple of people if they had any *bangi*, which was how they said marijuana in Swahili. Someone pointed to a couple of guys who were crossing the street. I went up to them and asked. They smiled and one of them pulled two bomber joints out of his pocket and just handed them to me. They said they could get some for us to buy but it would take an hour or more for them to get it and come back.

One of the guys lit a match so I started puffing on the joint, right on the spot. Before I could even start coughing from the smoke, I heard someone say, "Put your hands in the air," and, when I looked around, there were two guys, one with a handgun, who looked just like the guys who gave us the pot. But they were the police. They all were wearing black pants and short-sleeved white shirts; in fact, almost all guys around Moshi wore the same clothing.

These guys took the joints from me. "Start walking in that direction, to the jail," one said as they both pointed their guns at us. When we got to the jail, a couple of blocks away, the two cops spoke with the guys who gave us the joints and waved them off. They disappeared very quickly. We went into the jail and sat down at a small table. One cop did all the talking.

"OK, you want to leave? It will cost each of you 50 shillings." That was about seven dollars. Daniel started crying. I think it was an act but he was really good at it, I have to admit. They got tired of his tears pretty quickly and said to him, "OK, you didn't have any *bangi* on you. You can go." He got up and left, giving me a wink on his way out the door.

The cop turned to me. "You can also leave but it'll cost you 50 shillings."

"I'm a budget traveler and I don't have that kind of money." I had just spent plenty on a room for two nights so I didn't budge.

"The magistrate will be here in the morning and, if you're still here, he could sentence you to six months in jail."

I stood my ground. "I don't care. I don't have the money."

He walked me into the back and put me in the one cell they had there. Already inside was a young boy. He must have been eleven or twelve years old.

"So, young man, why are you in here?" I asked him.

"I was arrested for stealing a chicken from a neighboring tribe. My father died recently, bitten by a poisonous snake, and my mother had trouble feeding our family."

I'd heard of snakes killing people regularly when I was there so I was very sympathetic to the boy's story. There are green and black mambas and puff adders. Most of the people killed lived in small villages.

The next morning, the cop came, opened the cell door, and waved me out. He walked me to the front door and then handed the two joints back to me. "OK, you can go."

As I walked outside, he followed me and asked, "Would you like to smoke one of these joints with me?"

I was incredulous. "How could you keep me in jail all night then not only give me back my joints but have the nerve to ask to smoke it with me?"

He laughed. "It's not illegal to have *bangi* but, if you do it in public in the future, don't stand in the middle of the street and smoke it like you and your friend were doing. It's better if you stand on the sidewalk."

Shaking people down for money was an accepted practice so he didn't feel bad about his attempt in extorting money from me at all.

"Sorry," I said. "I'm not in the mood to smoke it with you right now."

*****

Brad and Daniel told me about Kanamai, a Christian convention center that was a hostel, situated on the Indian Ocean and just a dozen miles north of Mombasa. We decided to meet there, each going on our own. I hitched a ride to Tanga, the northernmost seaport in Tanzania. It was midday when I arrived and it was incredibly hot and humid. The town was pretty shabby where I was let off. The streets were of a red dirt and the whole place was dusty and full of trash.

I spotted an Indian restaurant across from the bus station where I'd just purchased a ticket to Mombasa, the bus set to depart an hour later. The restaurant had no air conditioning. It was cafeteria style and I walked down the line of pans sitting in steaming hot water with mainly meat and vegetable curries. I had no experience with curry of any kind so I pointed to one that looked like beef stew but which actually turned out to be chicken vindaloo. Just the hottest, spiciest, killer Indian dish on any menu. They served it with rice and the all-important pitcher of ice water.

Not only had I had no experience with curry but, at that time, I'd never had any food anywhere, USA or abroad, that had chilis mixed in. I was famished and ready to devour every last morsel on my plate. I took a bite and, while very tasty, I immediately noticed that the food had bitten me back. With sharp teeth. Wow! My mouth was on fire. I downed a whole glass of ice water and, after two or three minutes, I was able to breathe normally again instead of the intermittent gasps of breath I took while drinking the water down.

I was now sweating profusely, drenched from head to toe, and just leaving the tip of my tongue in a newly filled glass of water to continue the cool-down. Maybe five minutes of pain, all in all. I took another big forkful, making sure to get plenty of rice before dipping into the vindaloo. I got it down very quickly, hoping to bypass the sensitive taste buds still hurting from the first bite. I thought I did a pretty good job but, alas, the heat started in again and down went another glass of water.

When the pain subsided, I was about fifteen minutes into that meal and had a total of two bites of food and two glasses of water. At that rate, I'd miss the next four buses to Mombasa before finishing off the meal and I'd need an intake of 23 gallons of water. That wasn't working out at all. I left the restaurant and went to an open-air fruit stand and bought a few bananas. They had a few varieties and, unfortunately, I picked one that, when I peeled it, I realized had seeds in. That was a real turnoff. The big clock indicated my bus was leaving in 25 minutes so I got on board, not being able to get out of Tanga fast enough.

While the bus traveled fairly quickly, it did make a couple of stops. The first time, there were a couple of guys tending a small barbeque grill on the side of the road. I was still pretty starved and I got out to see what they were cooking. There were 30 skewers or more on the grill and they kept applying some kind of sauce. It smelled great, whatever it was. I ate one and it was very good. At least it didn't have chili on it. I bought a few more and felt great from having some hearty barbeque. As I left, I asked if anyone from the bus knew what the meat was. Everyone was saying *paka*. Finally, one guy a few rows in front of me turned around and said, "Here, kitty, kitty."

The bus continued on its way, stopping an hour or so after we crossed the border going into Kenya. Again, there was a guy on the side of the road and he had a truck full of pineapples. Huge pineapples. Eighteen-inch-long pineapples. He cut them into nice, long, thick sticks and wrapped them in some paper. That really hit the spot. Sweet and delicious.

Finally, we made it to Mombasa and the sun was just about down. I walked a couple of blocks from the bus station and someone said there was a Sikh temple where people could sleep for free on the roof. I found it and went inside. I could smell marijuana smoke and just followed the scent up the stairs to the roof. There were lots of people up there, mostly hippies from Europe. It was a regular party and, after hours of hanging out and meeting people, we all just lay down on our sleeping bags and felt the warm night air and the swarms of mosquitos. The mosquitos weren't as much of a problem anymore. After a while, I just forget I was scratching at all.

KANAMAI

The next day, I found a bus going north and eventually got off near Kanamai. Once I got off the bus, I had to cross a swampy area and then I saw what I was looking for. There was a dormitory with several bunk beds and there were a few private bungalows. I was used to sleeping on the ground and there was a line of palm trees near the edge of the beach where I set up camp.

The hostel also had a cafeteria where you could get breakfast, lunch, and dinner, all at dirt-cheap prices, and an area where they had stoves, refrigerators, and private cabinets you could rent on a daily basis so you could cook your own meals. They were outdoors too so it was a very cool setup, allowing you to eat what you preferred and cook it in a social setting, with others cooking their meals alongside you. I had a meal in the cafeteria, went back outside, had a smoke, and lay down on my sleeping bag under a palm tree and drifted off, listening to the soothing sounds of the Indian Ocean's waves lapping the shores, not far from where I was.

That first night, I learned a valuable lesson. A life-saving lesson. Never sleep immediately below a coconut palm tree. How did I learn that? While I was in my dream state, I heard a loud crash. I wasn't sure what it was that woke me up. Was there someone there? Was it just a dream? I couldn't say for sure. In the morning, as the sky lit up, I looked a couple of feet to my left and saw a big coconut in its husk and then remembered the crashing sound in the middle of the night. If it had hit my head or chest, I would have been dead.

That morning, I saw Daniel and Brad. We had a great day, reliving our climb and our adventures traveling from Moshi to Kanamai. There was a soccer field and we got together with a few other travelers and played soccer frisbee for hours. Then we'd run into the water and get wet. The Indian Ocean in that area was very shallow due to a coral reef a quarter mile off shore. You could walk out for a hundred yards and it would still only be barely up to your knees. It was crystal clear, warm, and there were clear little buggers that would sting you. I figured they were from the jellyfish family.

The second day there, I met a very interesting guy walking on the beach with his girlfriend. As I walked toward him, he announced, "I know what you need," and he proceeded to open his daypack and pull out a binder. It was full of pages of clear, glossy dots, maybe a half inch in diameter. One hundred per page. He told me it was LSD made by a chemistry professor friend from a university in Southern California.

He tore off a page and handed it to me. He said two or three of them would be good for a few laughs and five would be major hallucinations. He himself was a professor of literature at the same college where his chemist friend worked. He then bid me happy trails and headed off.

On New Years's Eve day, I was sitting on the beach with Daniel and Brad and a guy with real long hair was walking up the beach with a big backpack. He asked directions to Kanamai and I told him he was there. He went to the office, signed up for a bed in the dorm, and came back down to the beach to hang out with us.

He had the same surname as me and said he was from Chicago. I was thinking there weren't that many Lisses so I figured we must be cousins somehow. Later in the day, around sunset, I told him I had some LSD if he'd happen to like some. I was just about to take five of those dots the guy from South California gave me. The cousin from Chicago said he'd be up for it and so the four of us took five each.

Next door, there was a bar disco and, as we started tripping out, the music from their big sound system had a Pied Piper effect and we kept moving closer and closer while still on the beach. After an hour or so, the stars were out in full force and the four of us were dancing on the sand. The hallucinations, with that black sky and the zillion stars as backdrop, were nothing short of fantastic. The feel of the sand at our feet and the waves gently crashing on the shore created a major sensory overload.

Sometimes, we'd lie flat on the sand, looking up toward the sky, and we'd try to describe to each other the visuals we were experiencing, have some laughs, get philosophical, and then retreat way back into ourselves, feeling and seeing the music.

Daniel asked me, "What do you see, Ken?"

"I see Jesus' face on a piece of toast. You have any apricot jam with you?"

Around midnight, I got up off the sand and saw Daniel and Brad but the Chicago Liss had disappeared. I figured he went into the dorm and crashed for the night. The next morning, the people at the office said he checked out with his backpack around 11 p.m. We never saw him again.

*****

Renting the kitchen facilities right next to mine was Denise, a Canadian nurse who'd been working in a hospital in Kampala, Uganda, for a few years but was forced out by the tyrant, Idi Amin. He banished all white medical personnel from hospitals and clinics during his reign. She was strikingly beautiful, a fair-skinned blonde. I watched her whipping up a meal to be envious of while I fumbled around with an omelet that only a very hungry person would even consider touching.

Denise was one of the sweetest, most down-to-earth, easy-to-talk-to, beautiful women I have ever known. From first look, I would have thought to myself, *There's no way someone like her would talk to me*. She had a face you would expect to see on the cover of *Elle* magazine, and platinum blonde hair. The smile though told me she was approachable. We instantly became good friends. We'd meet for meals and sunsets daily.

During the day, she was busy filling out job applications for work all around Africa. She didn't want to go back to Canada yet. She had plenty of energy to continue her work in a place where people could use top quality medical care. I really hoped she didn't get a job too quickly so we could continue our friendship indefinitely. After a couple of weeks though, she received a letter from a hospital in Botswana, telling her she had a job if she wanted it and for her to come down there as soon as she was able. So that was it. A great couple of weeks with a Canadian goddess. I was lucky to have spent any time with her at all so I felt pretty good, even when I had to say goodbye.

*****

During our stay at Kanamai, Daniel ran low on money so he went to the port in Mombasa and found a job as a first mate on a cement tanker that did a run from Mombasa to Zanzibar to Seychelles and back, twice a month. My recollection is the ship was called the MV *Southern Baobob*. Daniel was around only sporadically once he started work.

One day, we went for a ride on his BMW bike out in the bush. We were cruising along on a dirt road and his bike came to a quick stop as the back lifted off the ground for a moment and then came crashing back down with a real thud. Daniel was excited and pointed to the road. There in front of us was a huge monitor lizard, standing maybe a foot above the ground, and in its mouth was a snake. The lizard was turning his head in a way that effectively smashed the snake onto the ground. Finally, it ate the snake and, wham bam, it was over. The lizard must have been seven or eight feet long. A real monster.

Daniel made some great connections while working on that tanker. After I returned home later that year, I was to receive a series of letters from him. He met a guy named Ferrari in Mahe, the largest island in the Seychelle Islands, who had some kind of successful business there. During a meeting, he discovered Daniel was an accomplished sailor, having twice sailed around the Cape of Good Hope, a difficult task for anyone. He asked him if he'd like to deliver a three-masted schooner to him in the Seychelles from Monte Carlo where the boat happened to be. Ferrari said he'd provide an all-Italian crew to work the boat and Daniel would be the guy in charge.

He offered enough that Daniel was set to quit his job on the cement tanker. Daniel wrote to me, asking if I'd like to join him so he would have an English-speaking buddy on the trip. He said I only needed enough money to get there as he'd give me any spending money I needed during the five-month trip. It took that long because they stopped in ports all the way down West Africa and then up the eastern side and into the Indian Ocean.

I was totally stoked to do that trip. I had my ticket to fly to Paris and then to Nice which was just a short bus ride from Monte Carlo. Then the whole trip fell apart. Ferrari was convicted of some kind of felony in Mahe during the months Daniel and I were corresponding about it and Ferrari was deported back to Italy. The telegram I received from Daniel telling me the trip was off was the last I heard from him. I had his home address, sent a Christmas card, and his parents replied, maybe a year later, telling me their son was off working on a cargo ship somewhere.

*****

But back to Kanamai. With Daniel tied up working the majority of the time, Brad and I decided several weeks at Kanamai was great but it was time for a new experience. Lamu, an island and part of the Lamu archipelago in Kenya, was the place we decided on. The Chinese settled on the island after their ships sank near Lamu Island in the fifteenth century then the Portuguese invaded in the sixteenth and controlled trade along the East African coast. The islands of the archipelago were a group of 90 or so atoll islands, none of which were inhabited other than Lamu itself.

We took a taxi to Malindi to start the trip. On the way, the driver drove faster than we thought was safe, several times screeching his tires around turns. Brad and I were white-knuckled in the back seat. In the distance, we saw two local women with baskets on their heads starting to cross the road.

As we approached, they saw the fast-moving car and both turned back to where they came from. Unexpectedly, one of them turned around and tried to dash across the road, toward her original destination. The taxi hit her and knocked her in the air, flying her over the car.

When we came to a halt, the driver got out and ran over to her lifeless body and yelled at the top of his lungs at her. People nearby came over to the driver and pinned him down on the ground while others ran for the police. We had nowhere to go without a taxi so we watched the whole scene unfold. More and more locals crowded around the taxi driver and tried to get at him to kick or punch him. There were so many angry people so close to him that no one could really get a good kick or punch in. They were just all pressed against him.

Eventually, a cop car came and they pulled people away so they could reach the driver and put him in the back of their car, mostly to protect him from the crowd. They drove off and that was the end of that, although we were out of a ride. It took us a couple of hours to hitch the rest of the way to Malindi.

Before we got there, we came to a small canal, of which there were many as we drove up the road along the coast. We would have to take a ferry across. It was more like a barge, a flat, wooden structure that maybe ten or twelve cars could use at a time. On each side of the canal was a log coming out of the ground with a steel cable attached to it. That cable went through some steel rings attached to the barge. Everyone on board got out of their car or bus and went over to the side with the cable. We all had to pull on it to move the barge across the canal. To make it more interesting, as we slowly moved across the canal, in the muddy water, just a few feet away, were crocodiles swimming alongside us, just hoping someone would fall in. It was the same scene at each canal barge crossing.

In Malindi, which was a wonderfully laid-out seaside town with gorgeous white sand beaches, we found a beautiful park. It was really well groomed and, on the side above the beach, was an amazing campground with picture-perfect campsites overlooking the ocean. We sat and enjoyed the view and met and hung out with a couple of American guys who were with the World Health Organization (WHO). They'd been working for WHO for a year and were just starting a month-long vacation before beginning their second year of commitment. They traveled from village to village, inoculating the natives against smallpox. We drank a lot of beers with them and then just crashed on the lawn near their tent.

The next morning, we continued our journey up to Lamu.

Kanamai's campgrounds just north of Mombasa, Kenya.

Brad, Daniel, and me at Kanamai, just north of Mombasa.

LAMU

After a long, bumpy ride from Malindi, at least seven or eight hours, and a couple of pull-the-cable ferry crossings, we reached the ferry boat to Lamu, the oldest Swahili settlement in Kenya, constantly inhabited for over 700 years. The town looked old and immediately stood out from all the other places I'd been in Kenya and Tanzania in that the men wore full-length robes and the women black wraparound cloth common in other Islamic cultures. There were plenty of Westerners too as it was a hippie haven.

From town, it was a 45-minute walk to the most gorgeous of beaches, Shela, a seven-mile, white powder sand beach that was just dazzling and with incredibly clear, light turquoise water. When I got in the water, I could see the tiniest grains of sand under my toenails. It was that clear. It was the first time I'd ever been on a white powder coral beach. The sand was cool, unlike all the other beaches I'd been on, which were hot underfoot. It was so beautiful I could have lived there but it was expensive to stay at Shela Beach so we got rooms at the Pole Pole guest house in Lamu Town. It was dirt cheap and the mosquitos and bedbugs were no extra charge.

The rooms had mosquito nets, which were impossible to do without, but nothing could protect us from bedbugs. The room couldn't have been more than $1.50 a night. The parties though, night after night, were a blast.

After several days of walking the long distance to and from the beach, we found we could hop on a *dhow* — a crude, open-hull fishing boat — for next to nothing and then it was a ten-minute ride to and from Shela Beach. One day, the guy sailing the boat didn't quite understand where we wanted to go and, when we rounded the island, he veered away from our destination.

"Hey, mister, we want to have you take us to that beach over there." He wasn't listening and probably didn't know what the hell I was saying. After a couple of minutes and more protests by me, trying to get him to take us close in near the shore, I realized we were getting farther and farther away and knew we wouldn't win this argument so we jumped overboard and swam a long way to the beach. I thought my chest was going to explode when I finally felt the soft sand under my feet, walked to where it was only a few inches deep, and just collapsed in exhaustion while the water gently ran up over me. I think I got a ton of sand up my nose, lying there face down, but I didn't care.

There was a movie theater in Lamu Town, a small room with rice mats on the floor. Being a Muslim place, women sat on one side of the theater and the men on the other side. The movie, *The Cowboys vs. the Dinosaurs*, was a grade-B movie in English with subtitles and was hilariously bad. They didn't have popcorn either but you could smoke weed there so it wasn't a total bust.

After a few weeks in Lamu, as much as I loved all the partying with fellow travelers and the fun in the sun, sand, and sailing on the *dhows*, I realized my time there was coming to an end. Brad had met an English lady practically the first day we got there so I didn't see much of him. In fact, I left without saying *adios*. I just couldn't take the bedbug situation anymore. The bites were affecting my hands and my fingers were all swollen and causing quite a bit of pain. I went to the local pharmacy, hoping they might have something to help but they didn't. The only thing that would make a difference was to get away from the bedbugs so I said my goodbyes to some good friends I met there and took the ferry from town back to the mainland.

After traveling by bus back to Malindi, I went back to the campground we stayed at on the way up the coast. I headed to the same location in the campground and there was one of the WHO guys I met the first time.

"Hey, where's the other guy you were here with last month?" I asked.

He handed me a beer and told me an unbelievable story. "After you guys left, we traveled to Lake Turkana on the Kenyan side of Lake Rudolph which extends into Southern Ethiopia. The lake's rich in all types of edible fish, and crocodiles and hippos are common there too. We were enjoying a day swimming in one of the tributaries when, all of a sudden, I stepped on a sharp object and jumped to the side in pain.

"Just as I jumped to my left, I felt something rubbing the side of my right arm. I turned and watched it go by. It was a gigantic crocodile. It would have gotten me if I hadn't jumped to the side as it approached. The croc continued through the water and headed straight for my friend. I yelled for him to get out of the water but he'd only swum a few strokes and the croc attacked him, ripping him in half. It swallowed the whole top half of his body, with the legs left behind in the water, and it then swam away."

All I could say was, "Wow."

He continued. "I got out of the water and ran to a village nearby and told the locals what happened. They grabbed spears, headed back to the river, and took off after the crocodile, finally finding and killing it. Later, they cut it open to save the meat and found the body of my friend. I've been so depressed ever since." I could totally understand how losing a friend like that was unfathomable.

Lastly, he said, "I can't wait to get back to work in a few days and do my best to get the image of that scene out of my head, if that's going to be possible."

We were pretty much speechless the rest of that night so I just played some of my classical music, something that would ease our minds, mostly his, my favorite being *Scheherazade* by Rimsky-Korsakov. Later that week, I went back to Kanamai and spent another week or so relaxing on the beach. It was different this time without Brad and Daniel but my tan, after day in and day out lying on the beach from sunrise to sunset and beyond, was off the charts. My hands and fingers returned to being pain free and I was eating well at the cafeteria so I was very healthy.

While there, I met some people who talked about South-East Asia. It sounded wonderful and like it might be more comfortable and fun than what I'd been experiencing for those few months in Africa. I went down to a shipping office in Mombasa and found a cargo ship that was leaving the next day for Port Klang, Malaysia, also known as Port Swettenham. This was in central Malaysia, not far from Kuala Lumpur, the capital city. It was a good spot to head north to Thailand and other parts of South-East Asia or to head south to Singapore and on to Indonesia. I had enough money left over that I could afford to stay another couple of months once I made it there and have another new adventure.

I paid for my ticket and went back the next day just a couple of hours before the ship was about to depart. Just before I went through customs to leave Kenya, I took out my sheet of paper with the LSD drops on it and took my usual dose of five dots so I could have a party for one. The journey was supposed to take about seven days or so. I'd been traveling with Ayn Rand's *Atlas Shrugged* all this time and I'd finished it the day before. As I was walking toward the exit gate of customs, a young albino African boy walked up beside me. We talked and he spoke good English.

"So, brother, do you like to read?" I asked.

"Yes, whenever I can get a book."

"Well, here's one I just finished and I think you'll like it if you give it a chance," and I handed the book to him and immediately my pack felt better. I don't know if he ever read it but it was a good weighty object to finally be rid of.

As I boarded the ship, the purser, the person on every ship who's in charge of all money matters, came up to me, checked my ticket, and then took me to my cabin. What I saw wasn't at all what I expected. I was paying $30 per day yet my cabin was like a suite. There was a good-sized living room with a couch, coffee table, desk with chair, and then a bedroom with a large bed and a bathroom with shower. My LSD had totally kicked in and, after the purser left, I put away my few tank tops, shorts, and underwear, and locked the door to go up on deck and get some fresh air. After about two hours, I'd inspected every nook and cranny of the ship; at least, of the part of the ship that a passenger was allowed to go.

Suddenly, there was a tap on my shoulder. I was having trouble focusing on a conversation with all the colors and sounds coming mostly from inside me but what I heard, coming from this guy, really blew my mind. It was the captain of the ship. "Mr. Liss, there has been a change of plans. At the last minute, I was informed by our business office that there was a load of copper from Zambia and that we have to go to Dar Es Salaam, in Tanzania, to pick it up before we can head on to Malaysia. This means there will be a delay of at least four to five days, possibly longer if there are any complications. You are welcome to stay on the ship but, if you choose to stay with us, you will have to pay an extra $30 per day for your room and board." I was good at math so I knew immediately I couldn't afford to stay on the ship. "The ship will be leaving in two hours so please make up your mind what you want to do."

Getting my thoughts together was a real obstacle course but I made it through unscathed and asked him, "If I get off the ship and meet you down in Dar Es Salaam, could I leave some of my stuff in the cabin so I can travel light going down there?"

"No problem with that, Mr. Liss."

I got a few things together and disembarked the ship, still sky high. The purser got off with me and explained to the customs guy what happened and they cheerfully let me back into Kenya, which was just a case of walking through the gate. I remembered there was a pretty fun place, a large outdoor coffee house near Kilindini Road, where there were a giant pair of aluminum elephant tusks crossing the two-way lanes of traffic. I went there and sat at a table amidst dozens of tables. The atmosphere was perfect for tripping out. I always enjoyed a lot of activity when I was on acid, tons of distractions to keep me from getting all weird inside.

I sat there for what seemed like hours and finally realized I might like to try a beverage. Then I made a huge mistake, which I would soon be berated for. I held my hand up, looking at a waiter many tables away and, with my index finger, waved to him to come over. He stormed over, obviously angered, and, when he stopped a few feet away from me, he made the same motion I had made to him and said, "This is how we call a dog in Kenya." Oh wow, I felt so bad. Sufficiently so that I wanted to climb under my table. He said it loud enough that everyone at nearby tables stopped their conversation and looked over at me with disdain. The acid didn't help. It only enhanced my embarrassment.

After many apologies, I was finally able to get the guy to bring me something. I didn't dare look up at any of the other patrons, waiting for them to finish and for new occupants for those tables to arrive. After what seemed like hours, but mostly enjoyable once I was able to move on from my faux pas, I headed over to the Sikh temple to spend the night.

DAR ES SALAAM

I knew I needed to get down to Dar Es Salaam in Tanzania to be ready to board the ship once they were finished loading the copper. I figured I had three or four days. I was always very optimistic about things. The captain had said four or five days but I liked to think they'd get it done much faster. I got a bus straight through; twelve hot and sweaty hours to get there. The road was pretty decent but there's a trick to getting the most comfortable experience on any bus trip when you know the roads could have lots of bumps and pot holes — sit up front if you can. The back of the bus tosses you up and down all day, all night, Marianne. On the way, I frequently played Canned Heat's "On the Road Again" and always enthusiastically hummed along with it.

We pulled into Dar and I went straight to the YMCA on the recommendation of one of the travelers I met on the rooftop at the Sikh temple. He said it was cheap but as nice as any more expensive hotel around the city. They didn't have an empty room but asked if I'd be OK sharing a room with another guest who'd already checked in. I said I'd like to meet the person first. They took me to the room, knocked, and a very tall African guy opened the door and introduced himself as Mohan. He'd just finished his master's degree in gemology at McGill University in Montreal. He was A-OK to me as a roommate. We talked and talked for hours before turning in for the night. He was spending a week there before returning to his home in Tanzania.

The next morning, I went to the port and found the ship. I sought out the captain and, after finding him, he told me, "So sorry, Mr. Liss, but we've had a small delay and it's going to be about seven or eight days before we'll be ready to leave."

I had a dumb idea. "Well then, I've decided I'll start a fast today and will continue it until you tell me the ship is ready to leave. So, my health is on you, sir." Having a Jewish background, it was always easy for me to play the guilt game. He just laughed a little and told me to check back in five days or so. I went to a market and bought a large bottle of orange concentrate. This was what I would have three times a day, mixed with a large glass of water. I had a very difficult time that first day. My stomach

95

was growling and, every few seconds, I thought about stopping my dumb idea of fasting. Every direction I walked, I saw a restaurant, snack bar, or someone shoving some kind of food into their mouth. That's an exaggeration but you know how, when you break up with a girlfriend or a wife, every direction you look in, you see two people totally in love? Well, that's how twisted I was all day with the food issue.

I tried to pass time talking to people on the street. I was sitting on a bench on a pathway near a beach and a man sat down with me. He was a South Asian guy, wearing a business suit. "I'm on a lunch break from work and I only have a few minutes to get back but how would you like to discuss a business opportunity with me tomorrow?" he asked. "If you're interested, meet me here at 4 p.m. tomorrow." I told him I would. Now, one thing I was learning, albeit slowly, is that great things don't just fall in your lap so I knew I needed to be careful the next day. The rest of this first day was excruciatingly slow and that glass of water was anything but satisfying. I just knew I had to keep myself hydrated since it was very hot and humid in Dar. Somehow, I made it through that first day.

Every day after that, it was no problem at all. My stomach had shrunk enough that just the orange-flavored water was fine. I met the Indian guy at a restaurant the next afternoon. It was pretty bizarre. He was very well dressed in suit and tie and I was wearing my cut-off jeans and tank top. We met at the same bench and went to a restaurant across the street. He spent most of his time trying to impress me about how successful he was and laid down all kinds of ideas about new business plans. I wondered why he needed to tell me all this since it wasn't really very interesting. Then he hit me with the, "If you could give me $5,000, we could make a ton of money," line. I wasn't surprised as I figured he would get around to that. I let him know I was totally broke with no bank account at home to tap into. *Sorry about that! You just wasted time and a glass of water on me for nothing.*

*****

Each morning, I'd go to the port and look for the captain of the cargo ship I was waiting for. "Captain, take a look at me. I'm wasting away, waiting for this ship." He would laugh and tell me, "You look perfectly fine and don't worry, we should be ready to leave in another day or two at most." He'd always walk away, laughing to himself.

After leaving the captain, on the third day I ran into the English professor, Mr. Mayor, who gave me the page with 100 hits of LSD. "Hey, my friend, how did you like my LSD?" he asked me. I told him I loved it and that I'd given some to friends who'd also had a great time on it. "Tell you what," he said, "here's my business card with my P.O. box address on it. If you ever want more, just send me a note and I'll send it to wherever you are in the world at poste restante. Take care, I'll see you around again sometime." And he left, just like that. A year later I wrote to him and he sent me another 100. What a great guy and a real character. The world is full of them.

In the late afternoon on my second day in Dar, I was sitting in the garden of the YMCA and a really cute Japanese girl came up to me and started a conversation. Her name was Sachiko and she'd been living in New York City for a couple of years, working as a photographer's assistant. She decided to travel around a little before going back to Japan. She and I really hit it off. There weren't many single travelers in Dar and we found it a natural thing to hook up.

I was already a few days into my fast and, after another few days of it, the captain told me for sure we'd be leaving two days from then and I was to be at the ship by 5 p.m. I was ecstatic. We'd finally be setting off for Malaysia. After walking around the city for so many days, I knew exactly what I was going to do to break my fast but, before having my first bite of food, I wanted to weigh myself to see how many pounds I'd lost. I was really curious about that. I used the same scale I weighed myself with the day I started the fast. I got on and I was floored. I gained one pound during that week. I have never been able to figure that one out.

There was a bakery that had the most amazing cream puffs sitting in the window, freshly made daily. I went with Sachiko and bought something for her and I had two cream puffs. Unbelievably good, until the stomach ache started. I was doubled over with pain within moments after finishing the second cream puff. It took a couple of hours for that to go away. In retrospect, it wasn't hard to understand that I should have eaten something like broth with rice and eased my way back to putting food inside of me but hindsight is twenty-twenty.

The next afternoon, Sachiko and I were walking through the lobby of the YMCA when the guy behind the desk asked me to come over to him. He made a phone call and, five minutes later, two men came up to me, asked if I was Ken Liss, and then told me to follow them to some private room. They were Criminal Investigation Department guys, the CID. They started grilling me on my reason for being in Tanzania. I couldn't figure out why, after a week there, all of a sudden I was considered suspicious. They questioned me like I was a spy working for the CIA.

I told them what happened in Mombasa with the cargo ship and that I'd be leaving next afternoon. That wasn't good enough for them. They told me I had to be out of Tanzania that day. They said there was a flight on an East Africa Airways four-seater plane leaving in three hours and I'd better be on that flight or I was as good as in jail. They weren't flexible on this.

Sachiko and I hurried down to the port. I told the captain what had happened and he let me on the ship to get my belongings and wrote me a receipt and letter that I could take to his company's shipping office in Mombasa to get a refund for the money I paid for passage to Malaysia. Sachiko came with me to the tiny airfield.

I had my return ticket to Israel that I used as a voucher to pay for the flight to Mombasa. They gave me a voucher for that ticket, minus the cost of the flight. It was a tearful and unexpected goodbye between me and Sachiko, even though I would have left the following day on the ship. Up, up and away; soon I was back in Mombasa.

NAIROBI

After getting my money back from the shipping company, I was feeling down. I wasn't exactly sure what my next move should be so I went to Kanamai for a few days, lay on the beach, ate well, and came up with a plan to go back to Israel and head back to California. The money I had left just wasn't enough to keep going since my return ticket was from Nairobi. Not that I really had a return ticket anymore but, at that moment, I didn't give that any serious consideration.

I took a bus to Nairobi and, on the way, we passed through Tsavo National Park. After seeing Serengeti, Tsavo was no big deal but one thing that amazed me were all the termite mounds. They were everywhere to be seen along the route. They stood about six to ten feet high for the most part but I'd heard that, in some forested areas, they got as high as thirty feet on occasion. The structures are made by the termites using a combination of soil, mud, chewed wood, saliva, and feces. Seeing these mounds broke up what was otherwise a long and monotonous ride all the way to Nairobi.

When the bus pulled into town, I got off and, just a block away, was the New Stanley Hotel. The great thing about this hotel, which was way too expensive for backpackers, was their outdoor café. It was an excellent meeting place that was alive with everyone from the hippies like myself all the way to the well-to-do tourists outfitted in head-to-toe Abercrombie & Fitch safari gear, all prototypical big-game hunter folks who were mostly there for photo safaris. Their camera was the only thing they were shooting. Oh, there were some real hunters there too, gloating over their bravery and amazing feats. Assholes, all of them.

I sat down, ready to splurge on my last couple of days in East Africa. I ordered a beer. I rarely ever sat down in a restaurant or café during my travels to order something I could get for a third of the price at a local market. But this was the end of my East Africa experience and I was hot and tired after the long ride from the coast.

As I sat there nurturing my beer, I eavesdropped on the people at the next table, a guy with two women, very attractive women to boot. They seemed to be friendly at first, then there were some sarcastic words going back and forth before the two women got up and left. The guy shook his head when they left and I glanced over and casually, and with more than just a hint of sarcasm said, "Women, who needs 'em?" He reacted with a smile and asked if I'd like to join him. His name was Tom and he was from Toronto. A really good guy.

He bought me another beer and, when I started to gather my things and take some money out to pay, he waved me off and asked, "So, where are you staying in Nairobi?"

"Well, I just arrived here a short while ago so my next chore is to find a place to stay."

"I've a hotel room with two bedrooms so you're more than welcome to share it with me."

I was always in the mood for a bargain so I agreed to join him and we headed back to his hotel room. I walked over to the small porch he had and stood there, watching the sun setting, and then looked down below. On the ground floor was part of the hotel's restaurant kitchen. There was a large grill and on it were three pigs' heads. The cook went over every now and then to turn the heads so they seared evenly all the way around. It made me a little queasy to be honest.

Tom started telling me about his import/export business and then he opened a door in the room which went into an adjoining room. He had many cartons he said were filled with all kinds of curios bought in marketplaces around East Africa. He had everything from carvings to bead work to fetish dolls, hand bags, machetes, clothing, and on and on in these boxes that were already packed and waiting to be shipped. When I told him I was from San Francisco, he perked up, saying that was one place he'd like to open an African art gallery.

We talked about what and how he wanted to approach all this and he said, if he could find the right partner, he'd have him set things up in San Francisco and run the operation and he himself would just come out and visit on occasion and keep the inventory coming in. He asked if I'd like to be his business partner in San Francisco and I was certainly up for it. His main requirement was that I find a nice Victorian apartment in a commercial area of the city where the downstairs could be the gallery and the rooms upstairs would be where I would live and where he could stay when he was in town.

I figured around Union Street would be the best location. He opened a box that was ready for shipping and took out all kinds of cool carvings, masks, a great crocodile shoulder bag, and a few more things and said he wanted me to take this stuff back to San Francisco with me. I told him I needed more room in my bag so we decided I'd put two thirds of my clothes in one of the cartons which he would ship back there. Then he asked if I had some addresses of friends back home that we could ship this stuff to since the duty would be very expensive if we sent it all to the same address but, if we sent each box to a different person, we'd save a lot of money.

I got out my address book and we wrote out shipping labels on the boxes for at least ten different people. This made me feel very comfortable with the whole deal. Then he asked if I could share in the shipping costs since I was going to be a partner and my helping with the costs would show my commitment to the business venture. I had $400 left but only gave him $150 of it. A business partnership was borne.

Later that night, I woke up with chills and my body ached all over. In the morning, I was really out of it. I was shaking like a leaf and couldn't get warm, even while lying under extra blankets Tom brought to me. The next few days were a blur. I don't remember much of anything except Tom bugging me a few times to swallow something and drink some water. The rest of the time, I was totally out of it. I woke up properly eventually and looked around. There was Tom reading a *Newsweek* magazine. He was humming a song and then went on to sing the words, "You're so vain, you probably think this song is about you." He said there was an article about Carly Simon and her hit song in it.

He looked over at me and told me what had happened to me. "You were shaking so much, I got really worried so I had the hotel call a doctor to come to the room to check you out. He said you have malaria so he gave me some pills for you and instructions on how to take care of you. You know, Ken, you've been sweating a lot over the last few days and you should get up and take a shower."

When I got out of the shower and was drying off, I noticed that most of my moustache was gone. Tom saw me looking in the mirror. "Every time I looked over at you lying there, you were constantly chewing on your moustache. That's why it looks like it does."

He gave me a pair of scissors so I could even it out. Then I headed back to my bed, feeling very weak. Tom was out but came back in with a bowl of chicken soup from the restaurant downstairs and spoon fed it to me. I still felt weak but the soup really did me some good. Right away. After I was done, Tom looked over at me and asked, "Ken, can I sleep with you?"

I didn't get it at first. "Yeah, right, sure, of course," but I was kidding. When he gave me a look, I realized he wanted to have sex with me. I got a little tense and didn't want to insult him when I said, "Tom, I really appreciate your taking care of me and all his hospitality and I hope it doesn't ruin our African art venture but I'm not into guys."

I thought back to how the first thing I said to him at the New Stanley café was something to the effect of "Who needs women?" so it all made sense to me. He looked quite disappointed after I told him I was straight. He was rather subdued after that, not at all like he was on that first day. The next day, I went to the El Al office to make a reservation for the flight back to Israel, where my ticket home was good. I handed them the voucher I had from East Africa Airlines when they asked for my return ticket. They looked it over. "Sorry, but this isn't a return ticket. With this voucher, all you have to do is give us $600 and you can fly home."

"I had to use the return ticket to pay for my last-minute flight out of Tanzania. I don't have it any more." I told them my story. "If I had the cancelled ticket, would that suffice to fly back to Tel Aviv without shelling out $600?"

"Yes, it would. There's a warehouse with hundreds of boxes with cancelled airline tickets stored downstairs."

"Great, so show me where to start looking."

"We can't let you go down there."

"Well then, you'll have to phone the police because I'm not leaving this office until you give me a chance to find that cancelled ticket."

They finally relented. It was like looking for a needle in a haystack. I went through box after box and, in each one, were hundreds of cancelled airline tickets. Several times, one of the employees came in to see if I wanted to give up on this seemingly useless search. I was driven and I needed that ticket. Hours went by and finally I found a box with dates that were very recent. I got very excited, figuring I was now close to finding it. I still had to go through two more boxes of recently dated tickets. Finally, there it was! My ticket, the one I used in Tanzania several days ago.

I ran back up the stairs to the front desk and handed them the ticket. They just smiled at how persistent I was. They asked to see my student card which I'd used to get such a great discount. They looked at it and said the card wasn't valid anymore. I exploded. "What, after all those hours searching for the ticket, you're telling me this now?" They said my eligibility for student discounts expired a month ago, on my birthday.

I was really frantic. They saw how upset I was, had a short meeting in the back office, and came back out and said they would make an exception. I paid them the $100 extra that was subtracted from the El Al ticket to get the flight from Dar to Mombasa and, the next day, I was finally on the flight back to Tel Aviv.

Who coined the phrase, "Never give up?" Thank you!

RETURN TO CALIFORNIA

I flew back to Tel Aviv, looking forward to my last few days before heading back to California to make a few bucks and move on to further parts unknown. Well, unknown to me. When I reached Tel Aviv, I found an affordable hotel on Ben Yehuda Street. I'd stayed on that street before and liked the location. Right after checking in, I went looking for a place to eat and, lo and behold, coming straight toward me was my cousin Bernie.

"Hey, Kenny, when did you get back?"

"Bernie, just got in and put my stuff in a hotel a block away."

"Well, you must go get your things and come stay at my hotel with me. The Platters are here performing and I'm managing them. I told them I'm with CBS records. You have to meet them. They're great people."

I went and got my backpack and passport from the hotel and walked with Bernie to his hotel. They asked for my passport at the front desk, the usual thing when checking into the hotel, and said they'd give it back when I checked out. We went up to Bernie's room for a few minutes and then he said we should go meet The Platters. Before we went, Bernie said, "While you were in Africa, I left the kibbutz and ended up staying right where the movie *Jesus Christ Superstar* was being filmed in Israel. I became good friends with one of the actors, the guy who played Peter. And I partied with a bunch of the extras for a few weeks. One girl who was in the movie gave me this pair of jeans and I love them but they're too small for me. See if they fit you."

I tried them on and they were the coolest, faded denim jeans ever and with bell bottoms too. I loved them and they became part of my uniform. I hardly ever went out wearing anything other than those jeans for the next year, until they just fell apart. We went to The Platters' room and knocked. They invited us in and we sat and had a drink with them as they were getting ready to head over to the club for their show that night. We spent an hour there then went back to Bernie's room, feeling no pain. I took some acid I still had in my wallet and Bernie got ready to go to the nightclub.

He was always the prankster and, as I was really starting to trip out, he called to San Francisco where my dad was working. "Get Max Liss on the phone, please." My dad. The walls in the room were breathing and I could hardly collect myself when my dad came on the phone. He said something like, "Son, it's good to hear your voice. Where are you and why did you call?"

"Dad, I'm in Israel again. Just got back from East Africa and I'm with Bernie and he made the call. I didn't."

"Well, then let me get back to work. I love you and hope to see you soon. Please don't call me at work unless you have some kind of emergency, OK?"

Now with full hallucinations happening, Bernie and I took a taxi to the night club where The Platters were playing. We went up a long flight of stairs on the outside of the club. At the door was a huge bouncer. Bernie walked right by him and into the club. The bouncer grabbed him, pulled him back outside, and told him there was a cover charge. Bernie insisted, "Hey, I'm The Platters' manager. I don't have to pay anything."

The bouncer didn't agree and didn't like how Bernie said it so he pushed Bernie down the stairs. Bernie rolled down that long stairway, must have been twenty stairs. I couldn't believe my eyes what was happening right in front of me and had a difficult time knowing if what I was seeing was even real as I was hallucinating so much. I made it down the stairs somehow and Bernie winked at me and began yelling, "My leg, my leg."

Before we knew it, an ambulance appeared and they put Bernie inside and drove away. I stood there for what seemed like years and finally figured out Bernie was gone. I found myself a taxi and went back to the hotel and the breathing walls in Bernie's room. I waited and waited for him to return. I didn't see Bernie again though. The next morning, still no Bernie. I asked the front desk if they had a listing of hospitals around Tel Aviv and I called each one and asked in the ER had anyone come in with an injured leg. Nobody at any of the hospitals had treated a man named Bernie with an injured leg. I was dumbfounded and depressed. What happened to Bernie?

I called the airlines and made a reservation to fly home the following day. My favorite cousin had disappeared and I didn't want to be there anymore. I told the receptionist I wanted to pay for my room and they told me a very high amount.

"Why are you charging me so much?"

"Well, Mr. Liss, you were staying with Bernie and he informed us he was taking care of The Platters' expenses and he's not here so, if you want your passport back, you must pay us for Bernie's obligation."

I called Bernie's brother in the States and had him give me his credit card number. I then gave the hotel his number and then, after they'd run it to see if the funds would go through, they gave me my passport back. *Now, what do I need before I leave for the airport*? I went to a deli and bought a pastrami sandwich on a poppyseed roll and found a guy selling fingers of hashish. I decided to put the fingers of hashish into my sandwich to take on the plane.

We flew to Athens first. I ate the sandwich in the airport there. When we boarded the plane to continue on to London, I began to laugh hysterically, with tears streaming down my face. I laughed all the way to London and continued my laughing in the transit lounge there for four hours until the next flight which was supposed to land at JFK. There was too much of a wait to land so we went to Boston and sat in the plane while we waited for clearance to take off again.

Two hours on a runway in Boston, that's where the high from the hashish I ate began to tail off and I came crashing down hard. Finally, we flew to JFK and had a four-hour layover. It was incredibly hard to keep my eyes open. When we finally took off, we flew to Los Angeles and then connected to a flight to San Francisco. After almost 30 hours, I was home.

I slept for two days. This round of travel was over and I went to work.

CALIFORNIA TO INDONESIA

I moved in with my buddy Charlie in Los Gatos shortly after getting back home. It was spring '73 and I'd just finished reading Anne Rice's *Interview With a Vampire*. I was really inspired and decided I wanted to become a vampire. The main character in the book, Lestat, told the interviewer it was baloney that sunlight, garlic, or a stake through the heart killed vampires. He said many vampires live for centuries and then there's a time where the vampire cannot adapt to the times and that's when they shrivel up and die.

It's like an old hippie who keeps hearing rap and techno music and freaks out because music is no good anymore. Not like the "good old days" of the '60s and '70s. Maybe it's the fashion or the architecture or the invention of automobiles and no more horse-drawn carriages, but that's the end for the vampire. I considered myself someone who was able to adapt easily, having traveled to a variety of areas in the world having to eat new foods all the time, cope with different weather, etc. I could probably live for many centuries. So, I decided to become a vampire but I would have to ease myself into the blood-only diet.

I began with marinating my steaks at barbecues and then not putting them on the grill. I'd just sit down and eat the raw steak. That seemed the best way to go but I have to admit I grossed out a lot of people in the process. That idea lasted a very short period of time when I met my new girlfriend, Rhoda.

Rhoda was a comptroller at a university in San Francisco. I met her at a party at U.C. Medical Center and we had a great night. The next day, I called her. "Rhoda, it was great spending so much time with you last night."

"Ken, where are you living?"

"I live with my friend Charlie. Why?"

"Don't ask me why. Just get your things together and come on over to my apartment on 24th Street and Church Street. I'll be waiting."

And, just like that, I moved in with Rhoda after knowing her for one day. She was so smart and funny and beautiful, we would stay up all night, talking about everything under the sun and laughing and having sex. The laughing was before the sex, not after. We didn't sleep the first two nights. Not a wink. Finally, we made a pact we would actually sleep or we were going to be very ill, fast.

We had so much fun together. She was a big Joe Walsh fan and, when Barnstorm came to San Francisco, we went to see them play. It was at the time of their second album, *The Smoker You Drink, The Player You Get*, with "Rocky Mountain Way" on it. It was a great show.

Rhoda and I had a terrific game we would play. We'd make weed brownies, eat a couple, and then we'd get naked on her living room floor and plug two sets of headphones into the stereo. Then, while making love, we'd take turns playing different songs for each other. Sort of a battle of the bands. We'd be on the floor all night, enjoying the music, the high, and each other. We tried to play the game when doing acid too but we were so high we'd forget to put on music and, anyway, we were making our own music.

The night the movie *The Exorcist* came out, Rhoda's friend Bruno came over and we went down to the Northpoint Theater to see if we could get in. It had been getting great reviews so we arrived at 5 p.m., just in time to stand in line for two and a half hours until the next show. We all took some windowpane acid and stood against the wall of the theater, just tripping out while it rained hard and we waited for our turn to go inside. After two hours of heavy hallucinations, we went in and sat down. When the movie began, it was startling, right from the opening scene, and we felt totally straight. We all held hands for the entire length of the movie, we were so scared. When we left, the hallucinations began again. I never thought a movie could scare someone straight but that movie did it.

After a few months, Bruno asked us if we'd like to move into his house in Oakland. He owned the synagogue on Geary, right around the corner from where the Fillmore Auditorium was. He made it into a concert hall but, after a fire there, he had to close it down. He took the ten-foot high brass menorah and put it into his hallway in the Oakland house where it fit nicely below the spiral staircase. He also took two of the pews and placed them on either side of a long wooden table in his very spacious dining room.

Bruno's house was one with an open-door policy. His room was one everyone had to pass and he often had lovers over. While Rhoda and I walked upstairs to our bedroom, we'd have to pass his open door and hear and see a little of what was going on in his room. He was into S&M and always had the handcuffs and whips on display, hanging from a bookshelf in his room.

Rhoda had a friend come over one day. His wife was seriously at her wits' end with life and was suicidal. It became a very dark cloud over the house and that's when I decided I'd had enough. "Rhoda, lets split. I've really had enough of the craziness in this house and I want to go travel. What do you say? Take a leave of absence from your job and let's go see some beautiful parts of this world."

"Ken, I can't. I'm working on a new business idea and have to see it through. On top of that, I just got a promotion. I'll meet up with you though if things don't work out."

I remembered, before I had to quickly leave Tanzania and not take that cargo ship, how much I was really looking forward to going to South-East Asia or Indonesia. I decided I was going to fly to Jakarta, Java, and see what Indonesia was like.

*****

It was spring '74. Rhoda had told me that, if she lost interest in her job and missed me enough, she'd take a leave of absence and join me in Indonesia. I'd chosen somewhere I knew nothing about as I'd felt a great sense of adventure being in distant places and not knowing much about them beforehand. I called the Indonesian embassy and asked if there was anything I should know if I wanted to travel there. They told me I had to cut my hair if it was long. They didn't let hippies into Indonesia. I had pretty long hair, way past my shoulders, but the day before I left, I had it cut very short. Above the ears short. What a mistake. Shortly after arriving in Jakarta, I saw Aussie and Kiwi hippies everywhere. I felt like I was only half of me but I was there so I figured let's just have some fun.

I immediately decided Jakarta sucked; it just wasn't where I wanted to be. I'd met some travelers who'd said their next destination was Surabaya on the north coast of Java which was a good stopping point on the way to Bali. Bali? That sounded like something from a movie. I'm telling you, I knew nothing about Indonesia. No Google to go research it.

I took a long, long bus ride to Surabaya. At the bus station, there were dozens of trishaws, bicycles with a seat for two behind the guy peddling the bike. This was the Indonesian version of a taxi or at least the cheapest way to get around. Every trishaw driver yelled at you to get into theirs and immediately I was immersed in a wave of confusion trying to pick one. I chose a guy who looked trustworthy and asked him to take me to a cheap hotel close to where the action was. I took a room in a pretty dingy place which right away influenced me to get to Bali sooner rather than later. I'm sure Surabaya is a city one can enjoy for a while but paradise was looming in my mind and imagination and I really wanted to get there.

I do remember one incident in Surabaya that was a bit of fun. I walked into a bank to change some traveler's checks. I arrived at the window and there was a buzz going on in the background. People were crowding together, looking over at me. The teller even went back to them and they conferred for a minute before he came back and asked if they could all have my autograph. That really took me by surprise. "Who do they think I am anyway?"

The teller said, "You're Ringo Starr, aren't you?" We all had a good laugh and a couple of them came from around the counter and took a picture with me, even though my passport said differently. With that new head of short hair, being mistaken for Ringo didn't exactly build my confidence.

I left Surabaya with great enthusiasm. It was a bus trip that left around 7 p.m. and, although the bus was comfortable enough, there was loud music blaring and all I wanted to do was sleep and wake up the next morning at the beach. That wasn't exactly how it worked on those Indonesian bus trips though. About ten or eleven at night, just about the time you'd acclimated to the loud music and bumpy ride and were finally drifting off into dreamland, the bus pulled up into the parking lot of a roadside diner and they made everyone get off.

With the price of the bus ticket, you got two meals, whether you wanted them or not, so we filed into the place and an assortment of plates of curry, rice, noodles, and some pork buns came to our table. This wasn't what my palate was familiar with at that time of my life and only parts of the pork bun and a few noodles were enjoyed. I was hot, tired, and cranky, and trying to force down food I'd never tried in my life up until this point and I wasn't appreciating it yet. Little did I know just how much I would come to enjoy these foods eventually.

Twenty minutes later, we were back on the bus but again, just when I was about to fall asleep, we stopped, this time to take the ferry from Java to Bali. I don't know exactly what time it was but certainly the early hours of the morning. After the ferry crossing and a few more hours, we made it to Denpasar, the capital of Bali. *Now where do I go*? Denpasar was a sleepy city, much less hectic than Surabaya, but there was certainly no beach there. A sign said "*bemo* to Kuta" and, when I asked someone, they told me Kuta Beach was the place to be and a *bemo*, minibus, would take me there.

That's all I need to know. Paradise, here I come.

I just couldn't cut it.

KUTA BEACH

I got off the *bemo* after a most unusual ride from Denpasar to Kuta Beach, stopping among beautiful terraced rice paddies and flat terrain as well, every quarter mile or so. Each time we stopped, the young man riding passenger up front would get out and run over to a small roadside shrine with a flat container filled with flower petals. I later found out this was to honor the gods and for safe passage. They do this in both directions and never miss a stop. The *bemo* was like a small pickup truck and the passengers sat on one of two bench seats in the back with their knees pressed against the knees of the person opposite, while holding whatever bag, backpack, or luggage they might have on their lap. You got to know people pretty quickly in those close hot quarters.

After I got dropped off in Kuta, I felt hot, tired, and exhilarated seeing the lush jungle foliage all about with a small quiet beach town carved out of it. It wasn't too hard to point myself in the right direction and I headed down to where more action was on the main street leading to the beach.

There was a flurry of activity with travelers from all over sitting in open-air cafés and restaurants, and I passed wildly colorful curio shops with all kinds of cheap batiks hanging off racks inside and outside. Sarongs, blouses, and shirts of every bright color were jumping out at me but all I wanted was to find a place to stay and put down my two daypacks. I was traveling light. No huge bulky backpack like I had in East Africa the year before. The daypacks were pretty light and I knew I didn't need to take all that much with me as I could find almost anything I needed right there. I had a couple of pairs of shorts and several tank tops and ended up hardly using the shorts at all since I discovered the comfort of a sarong almost immediately.

I found a *losmen* (hostel) that had a room available that was very spare, to say the least. It went for about $1.50 a day and it had a bathroom. Well, a bathroom of sorts as the wall separating the bathroom from the bedroom area didn't go all the way up to the ceiling. There was a space about three feet below the ceiling on the two walls so any odor from that bathroom could drift over the wall and fill the whole room. This wasn't a sophisticated bathroom either. There was no toilet. There was no shower.

113

There was a small tub, too small for anyone to get into. There was a water spigot over the tub and a plastic, one-gallon-sized bucket for throwing water over yourself to take what they called a dip bath. Pour water over yourself, soap up, and then pour more water over yourself until free of soap and hopefully the dirt too. It was always room temperature since they had such warm weather all year so there was no need for hot and cold water.

The idea of no toilet wasn't a problem since I'd been in Europe a couple of years before and saw many public restrooms that just had the hole in the floor that you would squat over. It's actually a pretty comfortable position once you get the squat down. Once you "go," you pour water from the bucket over the hole until you wash it all down. They don't use toilet paper in these things either. You just wash yourself after you're done. It reminded me of a passage from Jack Kerouac's *Big Sur* where he spoke at length about the fact Americans have the dirtiest assholes in the world because, unlike a huge part of the planet that washes their butts after defecating, Americans take paper and smear the leftovers around. Not really very clean when you think about it…

The $1.50 per night also included a thermos of tea and a bowl of black rice pudding with shredded coconut and sliced banana, topped with condensed milk, sitting on a small table on the porch in front of your door each morning. The workers at the *losmen* would notify the kitchen when they heard stirrings of the guests waking up so that the rice pudding would be good and warm when you came out of your room. It was such a pleasant way to start the day. One by one, people would come outside their rooms and you'd get to see, and gradually know, some of the people who were staying at the *losmen* along with you.

For me, the order of things for each day was to head over to the main street, sit in a café for a while, sipping more tea, and then head down to the beach. Right away, I found myself a great batik sarong which acted as my beach towel all day. On the beach were always lots of vendors hawking arts and crafts, snacks, and cold beer. There was one favorite girl who had a bucket with ice and two beers in it. Without fail, she'd come up to me every half hour to see if I was ready for a beer. I was there for three months and every day she was there, like clockwork. And, along with each passing, she'd smile the biggest smile you'd ever want to see.

After a few days, I noticed some patches of bites on the back of my arms, my back, and the back of my legs and they itched like hell. I knew it had to be mosquitos so I went to a store and bought some mosquito coils to burn in the room. The wall in the room stopped short of the roof by about six inches in places to give good ventilation. It also let the mosquitos in to hunt you down, or out, if your dreams came true. Rarely in the tropics do the mosquitos leave any room I've been in. There must be something about

114

the combination of Russian and Romanian blood that drives them to me.

So that first night, I burned a coil and, to make doubly sure I wouldn't suffer any more bites, I slept under the sheet against the mattress. The bed only had a sheet and no blankets since it was never much less than 80 degrees at the coolest time of the day. The next day, I woke up and the raised patches of red skin were much larger and intensely itchy. I just couldn't figure out how those mosquitos got through the sheet to get me. I mean, I covered every part of me and even covered most of my face, only letting my nose poke through to get some air. Believe me, this wasn't a comfortable night's sleep, trying to hold a sheet over my face while sleeping.

I was really tired the next day and found myself scratching vigorously, pretty beside myself emotionally. I'd had enough and took a *bemo* to town and to the local hospital emergency room. The doctor examined my huge areas of red raised skin, on my back, arms, and legs. He then asked me a question that caused me to almost flip out. "What kinds of foods have you been eating?"

I snapped back at him, "Do you think this problem I'm having is some kind of allergy? Look at these red areas. These are bites, doctor!" He left the room, came back, and gave me some medication to take home with me. I threw it away as soon as I left the hospital. I returned to my *losmen*, found a spot in the shade, and just sat there and tried with all my might to not scratch anything. It was so hard to keep my hands away from those areas. While I was sitting, one of the ladies who cleaned rooms there saw me sitting, tears rolling down my face. I pointed to the bites and she said she knew what it was.

She went into the room and pulled my mattress into the courtyard and into the hot midday sun and left it there for a half hour. Then she came back and knelt down and picked something off the side of the mattress. Actually, she picked three things off. She came over and showed me. She said, "Bedbug." She took the mattress back into the room and told me I'd never have a problem with them again. But the damage was done. For the next three months, the bites on my lower leg and ankles would become a big problem. I had scratched so much already, I had a couple of areas where I broke the skin. I'd never heard of tropical ulcers but I had the beginning of them on both lower legs.

Turns out a break in the skin back home in relatively low humidity and cool weather makes it easy for your skin to develop a nice scab, which allows for healing underneath. In tropical locales, where you not only have a ton of humidity and hot weather but also lots of time swimming in salt water, scabbing is a very difficult proposition for your skin. Thus, the openings fester and they slowly get larger and larger, with the chance of

115

infection very high. The fact that I felt I was safe from those bedbugs who must have just celebrated when I slept under the sheet, having the time of their life eating away at me, gave me a protective feeling.

*****

I was soon off and running, enjoying the most of what Bali had to offer. Maybe my favorite thing was an endless supply of magic mushrooms. The Garden Restaurant became a regular hangout. They actually served magic mushroom omelets. They were on the menu; regular and large. I just couldn't help myself and went over to the kitchen and asked the cook, "What's the difference between the regular and large magic mushroom omelet?"

"The regular, with one handful of shrooms, would provide colors and the large, with two handfuls of shrooms, would make the earth move." Well, it was no contest. Nothing can beat having the earth move when in paradise or, for that matter, anywhere you happen to be. So naturally, I ordered the large. This was a learning process. That first large omelet I had was made with four eggs and garnished with lots of slices of cucumber. I was so stuffed, I had trouble making my way through the whole plate of eggs and shrooms but, being the trooper I am, I got it all down, like my life depended on it. I mean, it took such a prolonged effort to finish it, I was already starting to hallucinate before I even left the restaurant and just paying the guy was an ordeal in itself.

The song "Dazed and Confused" by Led Zeppelin came to mind while I was trying to figure out how to pay. I finally made it out the gate and onto the main street and all those shops with the colorful batiks were just talking to me. They were like a Broadway show, dancing and singing songs. The jungle was breathing in and out and luring me on toward the beach. The world was totally moving. I made it to the beach, took off the sarong, and from my daypack I pulled out my one-speaker cassette player and put on whatever tape I could grasp. The sun was setting and the colors were wonderful.

I stood up and went into the water, looking back at the beach with the jungle swaying. I could see young Balinese guys tossing frisbees back and forth and the whole scene was just too good to be true. I caught a few waves and then went back onto the beach and sat down and watched the scene as I listened to Rimsky-Korsakov's *Scheherazade* and just fell in love. Not with anything in particular, just having the most wonderful time and life was the most luxurious dream. The music wasn't the typical thing most travelers listened to but it did attract a number of people who were also

116

tripping out and who gradually moved closer and closer to where I was sitting so they could enjoy it with me. What an amazing afternoon and sunset.

When I could actually get it together to gather up my stuff and take steps forward and walk again, I went back up the road from the beach. That's how high I was. At the first café I came to that had some music playing, I grabbed a table and chair and sat there for hours until the place was closing down and I was coincidentally coming down from the shrooms. I knew from past experience that you can't do psychedelics two days in a row and get high so I didn't do any the next day and that was my new pattern for the eleven weeks I was there. I did the shrooms every other day an hour or so before the time the sun would start setting so I could trip to all those extra colors, body surf, and enjoy music, people, and being away. Far, far away. No feeling like it in the world.

The family who ran the *losmen* I stayed at.

Even in the Land of Smiles they have rules.

My neighbors in the room next door.

Locals selling their wares.

The Garden Restaurant where they would make magic mushroom omelets for you.

MAGIC MOMENTS IN BALI

Now I've established that eating mushroom omelets before enjoying the last hours of the day down at the beach was a favorite endeavor of mine, I'd like to reminisce about a few of these times that stood out above the others. Every month, I came to discover, there was a full-moon festival. One thing you have to remember is that there is some kind of celebration in Bali what seems like every other day. They celebrate pretty much anything you can possibly imagine. I would be willing to bet there's some place on Bali where they are celebrating that grandpa had a solid stool today. A very colorful and eventful society.

There I was doing my usual thing, body surfing while the sunset was starting to get up and running, and just standing in the water looking back at the beach observing the frisbees flying back and forth into the hands of acrobatic Balinese guys while the sky above the tree line was continuously alternating colors. Behind the flying frisbees was a broken white line following it all the way to the end of its flight and, when the guy who caught it threw it back, the broken line would intersect with the previous one, over and over again.

All of a sudden, I saw a few men with loincloths walking onto the beach, holding lit torches with big balls of fire rising from them. More men with torches came out of the jungle and formed a line from near the water's edge, out in two directions; like a V with the pointed part at the edge of the water. There must have been 30 or 40 of them. Women, looking so beautiful in colorful sarongs and blouses, came onto the beach with huge piles of fruit on their heads and they alternated with the guys with the torches, the V stretching all the way to the tree line.

Guys with musical instruments showed up next and started playing their traditional-sounding music but one with a good beat to it. A few of the guys with torches went into the middle of the V and started dancing to the beat, waving those torches around while the sunset was blazing. They stayed for hours into the night with the dancing and music and lots of Balinese from the village all crowding around, enjoying the festivities. It was a total party. They did this every full moon.

123

I heard there was a crater near the town of Kintamani and decided to take the long bus ride there, winding through jungle and gaining elevation. I got off the bus at Penelokan and walked toward the crater, passing a small lodge before sitting down on a bench nearby. A couple approached and asked if they could join me. One was Murna, a Balinese guy I'd seen in Kuta, a small guy with really long hair. All the travelers liked him, especially the ladies. The girl with him was a strikingly beautiful Aussie named Patricia. She had long brunette hair and was much taller than Murna. I had a bag of shrooms and asked if they'd like to partake. They said yes and I split them among us.

I had my cassette player and Murna offered an unmarked homemade cassette he said was his absolute favorite. I put it in the player and realized it was Pink Floyd's *Dark Side of the Moon*. I had other cassettes but we listened to this one over and over again while we sat there laughing for the rest of the day.

Inside the crater below was a cone-shaped volcano, Mount Batur. It had puffs of smoke coming out of it which really added a lot to the peaceful vision before us. There was a big lake on one side of the crater floor and, next to it, was jungle. As the jungle rose up a slope to Batur, it was pretty much all black. We were told there was an eruption there not that long ago, around 1967, when many people from the village nearby were killed. It seems it's good luck to not run from a volcanic eruption but, good luck or not, many died.

The scene in front of us was unlike anything I've ever seen. The crater floor, with the volcano rising inside it, was very large; about four miles wide and five or so long. Off to one side was another large volcano looming behind the crater, Mount Agung. When our day of frivolity and awe was over — I mean, when the sun went down and the fact that we were at pretty high altitude as compared to that of Kuta Beach — it got really cold. Rather than stand around looking for a bus that might never come, we went over to the small lodge there and took a couple of rooms.

After cleaning up, I went out to their restaurant. In walked Murna and Patricia, looking refreshed. We sat down and ordered some food. A guy at the next table, sitting alone, leaned over and started up a conversation so we asked him to join us. He was older, probably in his mid 30s. Not a hippie type at all but pretty straight-looking and wearing slacks, dress shirt, and sweater vest. He told us he was on holiday from his job in Singapore where he was the deputy ambassador, second rank, at the American Consulate. We were impressed.

"What were all of you laughing about so much when you were sitting

124

on the bench?" he asked. "I could see you from a distance when I arrived that afternoon." I told him about the magic mushrooms. He said, "I'm sort of curious what it feels like to be on magic mushrooms?"

"If I see you back in Kuta Beach," I told him, "I'll take you to the Garden Restaurant so you can satisfy your curiosity. How does that sound?" Sure enough, two days later I was sitting in the Garden Restaurant finishing up my omelet and in walked the deputy ambassador. (By the way, after that first time eating those four eggs and struggling with that amount of food, I told the chef he should only put two eggs in the omelet with the two handfuls of mushrooms. It was much easier to get down that way.)

The deputy came over and sat next to me. "If that's what I think it is, I'd like to try some."

I asked him, "Have you got high in the past?"

"Yes, I have, actually," he said.

"OK, I'll be right back."

I went over to the chef and ordered one of those "earth moves" kind and, before I knew it, Mr. Deputy had wolfed it down. We started walking down the street and, out of nowhere, he told me, yes, he'd been high; he'd smoked a joint twice.

"Twice? Nothing else?"

"Nope, just a joint twice."

Uh, oh. I was worried but didn't tell him. We ambled into curio shops to browse as we made our way down the road toward the beach. I was looking at some rack with sarongs on it when I heard hysterical laughter from another part of the shop. It was Mr. Deputy laughing his head off. We continued down to the beach. I put down my sarong and he, his towel, and went straight into the water. A great wave was coming and I suggested we give it a go. He nodded in the affirmative. I got a pretty decent ride and looked next to me. He wasn't there. I looked toward the beach. Maybe he took it all the way in. Nope. I didn't see him there either. I turned and looked back and there he was in our original spot.

I made my way out and asked him, "Bro, how could you miss such a great wave?" He seemed to have a hard time responding. He was sort of frozen in that position, looking at the scene on the beach and the sky turning different colors. I told him, "You really should try and catch the next wave. It's so exhilarating; you'll love it." Again, he didn't move. I went over and grabbed him gently by the arm and walked him back to the beach. He wasn't talking at all, just looking around with an occasional smile. I felt a little better when I saw the smile but was still wondering if he was able to handle what he was going through.

We listened to a couple of tapes including my *Blind Faith* tape which included, "Can't Find My Way Home." I also had a great Kenny Rankin live at the Record Plant that I taped right off the radio before I left for this trip. It was fantastic with his schmoozing with the audience between songs. He was funny and had the sweetest voice. When it got dark, I noticed music playing somewhere in the jungle. We walked toward that music as if being led by the Pied Piper.

It turned out to be a restaurant. If I remember correctly, it was called Poppies. There were lots of tables with palm trees all around with speakers attached to the tree trunks. How pleasant that was. Mr. Deputy said he was starving. He ordered not one but two meals, saying again how hungry he was. They brought us cold beers and the food. I was able to struggle through one meal and by no means did I finish it but I did have a good portion of it. Mr. Deputy's eyes were bigger than his stomach. In fact, he had no stomach at all. He didn't get one bite down. He sipped his beer and his head swayed back and forth to the music as his two entrées got cold. Well, as cold as anything can get in that warm balmy nighttime weather. We had a couple more beers, with hardly any conversation, before we left and headed in different directions back to our lodgings.

The next morning, I was in Made's café and Mr. Deputy walked up to me, dressed in suit and tie. "I'm getting a *bemo* back to Denpasar in a few minutes and then flying from there back to Singapore."

"Are you angry with me for what I put you through yesterday? I thought maybe you were higher than you wanted to be."

"On the contrary, I wanted to say goodbye and thank you for taking me on the most fantastic ride I've ever experienced. It was one of the two best days of my life, along with when I lost my virginity." He laughed. I was so relieved. I thought when I first saw him he might have me arrested or something equally bad. "If you ever come to Singapore again, Ken, make sure to look me up," he said and he gave me his card.

Too much, was all I could think.

*****

The other time that stands out among the better magic mushroom moments was one day, when sitting on the beach with the sky doing its color transformations and the music adding to the moment, I got a tap on my shoulder. Lo and behold, it was that vision of beauty, Patricia, the Aussie that was with Murna at Penolokan.

"Do you mind if I join you?" she asked, sitting down real close. I didn't quite put two and two together immediately but, in retrospect, it's obvious she decided she wanted an evening with me and was now making it happen.

I was all too eager to oblige. We sat and enjoyed the last moments of sunset and then she asked, "Would you like to go get a drink?"

As we walked up the road from the beach, there was a vendor with a folding table and, on it, three dusty unopened bottles of liquor. One was Bacardi rum. She picked it up, paid the guy, and then said, "We should go find some Coca Cola and bring it back to my room." I always liked a lady who knew what she wanted and didn't beat around the bush. That would be my job, soon enough. Ba doom boom. I spent the night and I walked out of there the next morning, as happy as a clam. Thank you, Patricia, for choosing me.

Murna with his mom and brothers.

Down inside the crater at Mount Batur.

NEW FRIENDS

Bali was a great place to hang out and meet people from all over the world. First, I met Andy and Linda, Canadians in their country's version of the Peace Corps. They were both stationed in Bangkok and made it down to Bali for a month after their first year of service. They were staying in the same *losmen* and we would, almost to the minute, get up at the same time every day and meet outside on our porch, starting off the day with the black rice pudding. We'd tell stories about back home in North America and they told me a lot about Thailand, a place that I would see later that year for the first time.

They'd taken the bus ride up to Penolokan the same day I did the mushrooms with Murna and Patricia. They were pretty straight and didn't want to sit all day on a bench overlooking the crater like I had planned but wanted to visit the nearby towns and hike around a little. I recall seeing them in the restaurant that evening and Andy waking me up to take pictures of the sunrise early the next morning. Thanks very much, Andy. It was freezing out and I knew my lousy little camera wouldn't take very good pics anyway.

I loved a couple of types of fruit I found in Bali. Rambutan was one. When I first saw clumps of hairy red balls, I figured, "That's one thing I'm never going to touch." It scared me seeing them for the first few times. Then a guy at the fruit stand declared, while holding up a bunch of rambutans, "Who knew jellybeans grew on trees?" He peeled one and popped it into his mouth and then, after chewing the white meat off the large seed, he opened one up for me and popped it into my mouth. I liked it right away. I wasn't afraid of them anymore. Whenever I took a train or a cargo ship anywhere, I'd bring a big bag of them with me to snack on.

My all-time favorite though was mangosteen. It has a purple leathery look, not appealing to look at. But when you peel off that thick purple skin, you find a small round white ball of sections of sweet tangy perfection. I felt like I won the lottery discovering this fruit you would be hard pressed to find back in California. They're a seasonal fruit and, when it's the season, I want to eat these things all day.

We used to do a lot of breakfasts and lunches at Made's. Andy and

Linda weren't really big on the beach the way I was as they were both very fair-skinned and the Bali sun would destroy them if they sat there from eleven until three every day as I did during my first weeks there. I later realized it was better to get off the beach by noon and save myself, just a little.

An Australian couple I met really liked the beach at all times of the day, Brian and his wife. Her name totally escapes me but I remember being surprised at the fact that he had that typical Aussie sound to his voice and she had a Brooklyn accent. She was from Brooklyn and had moved to Australia ten years before and met Brian who, when I met him, had really long wavy blonde hair. We really hit it off and I'd see them each day on the beach and finally we'd go there together.

"Brian, you have great hair. I notice those things a lot lately. I had mine pretty long just up until recently." I told him the story of receiving wrong information from the Indonesian consulate in Los Angeles which had resulted in me having a very short, military style haircut.

Brian digested this story in between chillum hits of Sumatran weed mixed with Afghani hashish. He told me, "I really feel bad for you, Ken, hearing about that long hair you had and how bummed out you are about losing it all." He then got up and disappeared for about 45 minutes. When he came back, his long hair was gone. He had someone back at his *losmen* cut his hair so he could make me feel better. Wow, if that didn't win me over. What a great guy! We'd only known each other for maybe a week and look what a gesture of friendship he made. I wish I could have pasted his hair onto my head.

*****

Also staying there was another Aussie contingent, friends from Adelaide. Married couple Danielle and Rick and their two buddies from back home were on a month-long trip. They were great party people, always up for a good time, and the laughter was never-ending. Rick was the only guy among them. We did everything together. Well, not everything but we did a lot, hung out at the beach, went to different places to eat together, drank beers, and got high in the afternoons on the porch and, on a couple of occasions, went to the Garden Restaurant and did some shroom omelets. They even helped the people who ran our relatively new *losmen* do some landscaping.

"Hey, Ken, look what we brought back from the pasture for you," they called over one day. It turned out they came back with enough sod to put around a tree right in front of our porch, a sod of about six feet in diameter.

132

It was first thing in the morning so, when Rick dragged me out of my room after installing the sod around the tree, I was looking at about 100 mushroom caps that had grown in that sod overnight. He'd taken the sod from a cow pasture where most magic mushrooms usually came from. We started turning people on to the handfuls of shrooms that grew out of the sod every morning.

One evening, I had a great time at a Kecak Dance show along with my Aussie neighbors. We all took shrooms and had a private *bemo* take us to the temple where the performance was happening. We got out of the *bemo* and moved toward the performers, laughing at the silliest things or even nothing at all. I was trying not to look at Danielle too much; she was looking so attractive. Also known as the Ramayana Monkey Chant, the Kecak Dance is a theatrical performance where the dancers move and act in a dramatic way with every facial expression, movement, and costume all choreographed. Rows of circles of men wearing checkered sarongs sat around a traditional Balinese coconut oil lamp.

The moment the men started leaning back and forth and chanting "chak ke-chak ke-chak ke-chak," we all fell silent; we felt as if we were under the spell of ancient Bali. I think a few times I even forgot to breathe, I was so taken by the visuals and sounds. I lost track of time and, before I knew it, the show was over and we were so high from the shrooms and the performance, I think we might have flown home on the wings of Garuda, a bird depicted in the tale.

One afternoon, I went to visit Ulu Watu, a famous surfing spot. The day before, I'd heard stories in the cafés of Kuta about Corky Carroll, a world-famous American surfer, who had apparently messed up at Ulu Watu and hit the cliffs. He'd had to fly out afterwards because his wounds were severe enough that he wanted to get to a drier climate so they could heal easily. Open wounds in a tropical place like Bali have a difficult time healing with all the heat and humidity. I wanted to see the place where he crashed. Once there I could see how precarious it could be if a surfer wasn't paying attention to the walls at the end of the ride. It was a spectacular place and thankfully the surfers I saw that day didn't come close to that wall.

I remember a couple of fun moments with Rick and Danielle. On one occasion, after smoking a lot of hashish, the sweetest thing happened. I was yawning and sort of stretching and, with my arms fully extended, a small bird flew down and landed on my index finger. What a bold move for such a little creature. And it just stayed for a long time. Any encounter like that is always one of those times when people either say or think, "Awwwww."

The story of how I came to have the hashish is a good one. Occasionally, I'd take a *bemo* into Denpasar to cash traveler's checks at a bank as there were no banks in Kuta. One day while sitting there, an

133

American guy next to me asked, "Would you like to buy some Afghani Primo hashish? I have five ounces and I have to get rid of it because I'm flying back to Michigan, leaving Denpasar this afternoon. I'll give them to you for $100."

Everyone and their brother had those old flour sack shoulder bags. I mean everyone. So he pulled out five 3/4 inch thick patties wrapped up in what looked like Saran wrap, opened one, and gave me a smell. It seemed like what I remembered it to be from back home. Each patty an ounce.

"I want them," I told him, "and I'm on my way to the bank to cash some traveler's checks. I'll pay you when I come out of the bank."

"OK, that's fine. I'll be right here waiting."

I went into the bank but not before he put all five of those patties into my bag. Again, I told him I would be right out with the money. I went inside and did the transactions. It could have only taken me ten minutes. I came back outside and didn't see the guy. I stood there for a few minutes and then started walking up the street, trying to be as visible as possible for him to see me. I walked back and forth and then, when I didn't see him, it struck me maybe I should just grab a *bemo* back to Kuta instead of making a spectacle of myself with a bag full of hashish, walking up and down a street like I'm lost.

So I got into the next *bemo*, made it back to Kuta, and this guy was on his way back to the States and I'd just got myself five free ounces of the best hashish in the world. The party was on me for a long time. Weeeee!

Another occasion that stands out in my mind is with Rick, Danielle, and their friends. I was approached by a shifty-looking European guy with a French accent. "Hey, bro, would you be interested in buying some cocaine?" he asked. We spoke for a while. He showed me the bindle and I paid him $10 for it and took it back to the *losmen*. When I opened it in my room, there wasn't much of it so I just put it on my dresser and snorted it up. I went out onto the porch where everyone was drinking beers and I joined in. Within a couple of minutes, I was a little nauseous. I'd done coke in the past and I'd never felt nauseous at all. I usually wanted to talk to anyone about any subject for long hours at a time.

Everyone was joking around and laughing and *The Allman Brothers, Live at Fillmore East* was playing. It was a typical afternoon on the porch, except I not only had nothing to say but I could hardly keep my eyes open. I wasn't tired but I was in a sort of dream world. I wanted to enjoy the usual party yet I was looking at myself as a total outsider.

"Let's go get some *gado gado*," someone said. It's a great veggie salad with hard-boiled egg and thick peanut sauce poured on it. A terrific light meal, or starter if you're really hungry. I ate them all the time and they were a favorite of most travelers in not only Bali but all over Indonesia. We walked down the main road to the best café for *gado gado* in Kuta. While we were walking, I came to and felt wide awake and like my old self. I noticed though that my nose itched a lot. For some reason, my hand kept heading to my nose for a good scratch.

We reached the restaurant, one of those where you sat, legs crossed, on rice mats at a low table. We ordered, the food came, and Rick took my bowl and ate every last drop. He then pushed the bowl back across the table to me and everybody laughed. I was incredulous. I pleaded with him. "Rick, how could you eat my food just like that? Stop eating my food, Rick. Please stop!"

I felt someone shaking me by my shoulder. I opened my eyes and they said, "Kenny, the food is here. Wake up." I'd nodded out and dreamed the whole thing. Not the kind of sometimes scary LSD hallucinations but a very pleasant, relaxed dream. I kept wondering what was going on with me but I ate my food and realized that what the French guy had sold me was not cocaine, but heroin. Heroin makes you dream and makes your nose itch.

*****

Towards the end of my stay in Kuta, I got close really fast to Kim, whose family had a store in Kuta Beach. We would sit around in her hammock every day and cuddle. She gave me a cheesecloth bag with jasmine flowers in it every day and told me to put it under my pillow at night and dream of her. I hated to leave her but I knew it was time for me to head home.

The final good friend I made in Indonesia was an English nurse I met on the beach. Earlier, I mentioned the tropical ulcers I'd developed on my ankles and lower legs after the bout with the bedbugs the first week in Bali. The sores were festering and not scabbing over. It was pretty ugly and the nurse was sitting on her beach towel not far away from me and took it upon herself to come over.

"I'm a nurse," she said, "and I've noticed you have a bunch of tropical ulcers you're really neglecting. It could be really bad for you if you don't start doing the right thing for yourself. You must keep them clean, dry, and take some antibiotics. So, don't swim in the ocean, keep the sores bandaged, and wear socks so no sand from the beach gets in. I can give you a month's supply of a very strong antibiotic. Take them as directed on the bottle."

I couldn't thank her enough. What a savior she was; sort of dropped out of the sky. I took the tablets for the rest of the time I was there. When I got ready to leave, I realized my feet were so swollen, despite taking the medication, that I wasn't able to put on my sneakers. I flew home with just the same flip-flops I wore each day in Bali.

I immediately made an appointment with a dermatologist. He examined my legs and told me that, had I left it one or two days more, at best I'd have a good case of gangrene and be needing amputation of both legs and, at worst, I could have died. It's hard to take good care of yourself when taking psychedelic mushrooms every other day for three months.

I look back and thank my lucky stars that an English guardian angel touched me at a time of need.

Andy and Linda in front of the lodge in Penelokan.

Made and Murna. Made owned the café in the background.

Looking cool at sunset.

Brian and his wife.

In Penelokan, the morning after shrooming with Murna and Patricia.

Richard and Danielle on the right and their Aussie buddies.

I had a crush on Danielle from Adelaide.

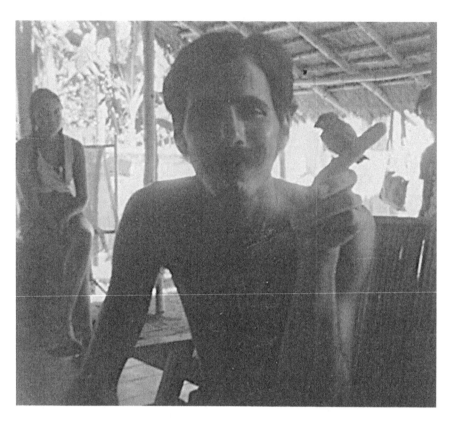

Showing off my feathered friend.

Richard and Danielle enjoying the shrooms.

Temple with the Kecak Dance underway.

Ulu Watu.

Downtown Denpasar. This is where the guy gave me the hashish.

SINGAPORE AND PENANG

I met Debbie in Mill Valley, California, after returning from Indonesia. It was the summer of '74 and I was visiting some shops in Mill Valley to try and sell some of the curios I purchased in Bali in order to raise enough money to get my next ticket over there. One of the shop owners was the wife of one of the Grateful Dead. She had some girlfriends there when I walked in and one, Linda, was particularly nice.

"Ken, come over to my house tonight to show your stuff to a bunch of my friends," she invited. I went and it was a great night with lots of wine and good weed and her friends bought a lot of my collection of Indonesian pieces. I went back to visit a few times over the next couple of weeks and eventually was introduced to Linda's younger sister, Debbie, who'd just got out of a stint in rehab having developed an addiction to Tanqueray and valium. She drank and ate those pills like they were cola and candy. Linda kept saying, "She's a great lady as long as you keep her away from booze at all costs. She has no ability to control herself once she gets started."

I was unsuccessful in keeping her away from it twice. The first was at a cowboy bar in Novato where she threw down five double tequilas when I went to the bathroom. When I came back, she was the only one on the dance floor, gyrating right in front of the band. I took her to a Denny's coffee shop nearby to get her away from the bar and, while we were standing in the waiting area, she bit me on the cheek and wouldn't let go. I could feel those teeth digging in. I looked around. People were staring as I pleaded with her, in a demanding whisper, "Debbie, let go of my cheek." She wasn't having any of it.

Finally, in total desperation, I slapped her cheek and she let go. I felt the blood trickling down my neck. The hostess was very thoughtful and brought me a couple of napkins to soak up the blood. Debbie was so out of it when the food we ordered arrived — a bowl of chili con carne for her and a burger for me — she pulled the bowl of chili toward herself and off the table, spilling it onto her beautiful dress.

The second time I failed to keep her away from alcohol was at my cousin Jeff's party where again she sneaked several shots and the rest of the night demanded I punish her since "she'd been very bad." She wanted me to hit her and I refused. I didn't want to hit her for many reasons. She wouldn't let up and started insulting me. She thought maybe she could piss me off enough that I'd become a violent angry man and exert some physical punishment on her. I didn't want to become that person.

The whole time this scene was playing out, we were on the front porch of my cousin's apartment. While guests were arriving, Debbie was lying on the porch, yelling at me to hit her. It's amazing nobody called the police as people had to walk past us and into the party. Finally, I gave her a couple of light slaps on her tush and she got up and said I was pathetic. That was OK with me. I just wanted to get her back home and get away from her. That's how dramatic and crazy she was if she had a drink. Maybe I was the crazy one. I kept going back for more of her.

Debbie had a lot of influence on her two sons, too. Bobby, the older of the two, was about four at the time. She brought him over to my mom and dad's house for Passover dinner with a big contingent of my aunts, uncles, grandparents, and cousins. We were all enjoying each other, laughing and drinking wine; that is, everyone except for Debbie. We made sure to keep the bottles away from her. The chopped liver was finished. So was the matzo ball soup.

All of a sudden, Bobby's little voice popped up. "Mommy, I want a glass of water." Debbie was engaged in conversation with one of the cousins. Again, "Mommy, I want a glass of water," and, again, no reply. To everyone's surprise, Bobby raised the bar. "Mommy, shut up and get me a fucking glass of water." First there was total silence. Then the whole group broke out into fits of laughter as Debbie took Bobby to one of the back rooms and gave him what for. It was never dull with her or her kids around.

*****

In the meantime, I was saving my money for an eventual trip back to Indonesia. Linda and her friends had a great idea — why didn't Debbie and I go to Singapore, buy up a bunch of Chinese silk, and have a load of cowboy shirts made that we could bring back to California and sell. Sort of a test run for a more large-scale push if it was successful. We finally set a date to fly over to Singapore together.

We took a Vogue pattern, the classic cowboy shirt, to have the tailors use on the first batch of shirts. We got a cheap hotel in Singapore and, as we emptied our luggage in drawers and shelves in the bathroom, Debbie noticed a plastic jar with pills in it. I told her my sister who worked for a doctor's office gave me 100 codeine pills just in case we had a need for pain medication. That was all Debbie needed to see. She told me she had a bad headache and obviously continued to have one for the following week because she took those pills two or three at a time, day in and day out, until they were gone.

It was pretty boring for me to watch her zoning out everywhere we went as she could seem wide awake one moment and, the next, nod out while standing and waiting for the light to change at a crosswalk. Mostly she just stayed in our room in her underwear to stay cool. Singapore was very hot and humid and our room only had a fan.

After a few days, I started spending a lot of the afternoons and early evenings at an outdoor café across the street from our hotel. It was a place where both students and businessmen would hang out. One day, while sitting with a few Indian students and drinking liter bottles of Guinness, one of the students pointed across the street and said, "Ken, look at that girl." There was Debbie in her panties and bra on the sidewalk.

I stood up and called over to her, asking what she wanted as traffic kept passing by. Debbie yelled back across three lanes. "Ken, come over here and fuck me!" The students got a big smile on their faces and all gave me a big thumbs-up as I walked across the street to take Debbie back to our room. I was glad to see her finally finish the codeine so we could get down to our task of buying the Chinese silk fabric for the shirts.

Eventually we succeeded and, having found a good tailor to do the job, we headed to Penang, Malaysia, to hang out for a month until our shirts were ready. We took a cheap room in the Pin Seng Hotel on Love Lane in downtown Georgetown. The first afternoon, we found a money changer to change some traveler's checks.

He asked, "Would you two like to smoke some heroin?"

"I really want to find some opium."

"I could get it but it'll take me a couple of days. How much do you want?"

I just threw out a number. "How about 50 grams?"

He said he could do it so we sat down with him at a café outdoors in a good area for people watching and he took out what looked like a very long coke spoon. He hollowed out the middle of a cigarette then poured some white powder, "China White" heroin, down the hollowed-out part. After twisting the end to close it tightly, using his finger he painted the whole outside of the cigarette with sweet coffee. He let it dry for a few minutes and then, when it was dry, he lit it. He passed it around to us and it was burning very slowly and evenly. It lasted quite a while and, after finishing, we felt a little nauseous but also pretty good at the same time.

He did another cigarette and we sat there for a couple of hours, drinking

151

coffee, sometimes talking, and other times closing our eyes and falling into a dream world. We were nodding like crazy. He told us, "There's a beautiful country mansion a friend of mine owns and if you two would like to be our guests for a really nice afternoon in the country tomorrow, come to this address."

He wrote down the address and handed it to Debbie. The next day, we got a trishaw to take us to this really cool house with a huge porch, just outside of the city. The money changer was sitting on the porch with a woman. They took us inside and up to a bedroom with a beautiful king-size bed and gave us one of the cigarettes. Debbie and I smoked it, got very high, and again the nausea hit us. We lay down on the bed and the woman waved a big fan, trying to cool us off a little.

She said, "If you take off your clothes, you will feel much better."

So, we got naked and the two of us lay there, holding each other and dreaming away. It entered my mind that maybe this guy and woman might rip us off or maybe something even worse but we were so stoned out from the heroin, we were pretty much helpless.

The woman left the room and, after a couple of hours, came back and brought us some tea. Then the guy showed up again and gave us 50 balls of opium that we'd paid for in advance the day before. We got dressed and out of there, feeling very lucky that there had been no foul play.

With a friend, just before meeting Debbie. I had just returned from Bali and loved my batik sarong.

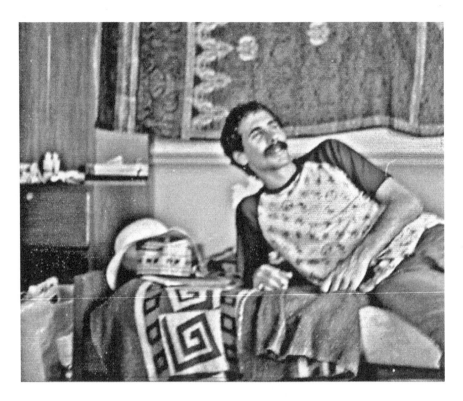

Georgetown, just after smoking the cigarette with heroin in it.

BATU FERRINGHI AND SINGAPORE

Debbie and I found a three-room, corrugated metal shack with a thatch roof in a fishing village called Batu Ferringhi. It was very cheap, something like $1.50 a day. It had a front room and two bedrooms with a plywood bed in each. The first day, we went into Georgetown and found a business that sold foam rubber and we got two four-inch thick pieces cut to the size of the plywood beds. Now we could lie down in some type of comfort at night. Or, as I did a few times, lie down during the day, too.

When I was in Singapore, I'd found a shop that made custom cassettes with whatever music you wanted. I really loved Blind Faith's "Can't Find My Way Home" so I had them make one tape with that song only, over and over again, both sides. It came in handy when I smoked one of those balls of opium and lay on my foam-rubber bed. With that song playing, I'd just lie there and dream away the hours. I loved beaches so much but my love for the "nod" was greater so I continued to spend days lying on my bed with the beach just several yards away.

These shacks had no air conditioning, or even electricity for that matter. There was a Coleman lantern in each room and an outhouse about ten yards from our front door. To wash up, we were able to use the bathroom of one of the families who lived near our shack. Nights were a real adventure. One of the corrugated metal walls in my bedroom was about eight to ten inches above the ground so, on occasion, I'd be lying there in my "nod" state, always with beads of sweat all over my body, and hear a chicken running in and around the room. I didn't bother with them. Eventually they would leave.

Both ends of the bed had walls and, all night long, I would hear the pitter-pat of hundreds of small feet which turned out to be geckos running up and down the metal walls. It was pretty unsettling knowing they were just inches away from my head but they never crawled on me so I didn't get too freaked out. It bothered Debbie more than it did me.

*****

Some afternoons, Debbie would disappear for a couple of hours. "Ken, one

155

day you should come with me to my massage appointment. I get them every day." The curiosity got to me so, the next day, we walked to a home in the village and a very tall and beautiful Indian girl with hair down below her butt came out to greet us.

"She's a real beauty, don't you think?" Debbie asked me. The girl showed us to a room where Debbie took off her clothes and got onto a massage table. The Indian girl stripped down to just her panties. I sat close by and observed. I was really happy Debbie suggested I came along! The masseuse oiled up Debbie and proceeded to give her a full body massage and, at the end, she performed some sexual favors on Debbie. I was almost foaming at the mouth to join in.

Finally, the Indian girl left the room and Debbie called me over to join her on that table and fool around. It was great. The visual foreplay was a new one for me. So *this* was where Debbie went on those afternoons. I really looked forward to the next visit.

That night, we went to a fun outdoor restaurant in the jungle and, just before we went, I ate one of the balls of opium. We sat at long tables and it was easy and fun meeting people from all over the world. Across from Debbie and me was an Irish guy and his English friend. After coming out of one of my many "nods" at that dinner table, I noticed Debbie and the English guy sort of locked in on each other. I looked under the table and they were playing with each other's crotches with their feet. I could swear Debbie had an orgasm at that table.

I was pretty pissed off and we left and went back to our hellhole shack. The next day was the day Muhammed Ali fought George Foreman in Zaire and we were able to watch the fight on a TV in a café nearby. After the fight was over, we walked back to our shack and I felt a wave of nausea come over me just a few feet away from our front door. I bent over and vomited onto the sandy ground. I looked at what came out of me and the food was very identifiable. The opium I'd eaten the night before had totally stopped my body from digesting the food at all.

While I was perversely enjoying that detail and feeling like crap, a commotion happened. About five or six chickens ran over and started gobbling up that food I was analyzing. Wham bam, it was gone, just like that. Immediately, I felt cramps and had to use the outhouse. Diarrhea took hold and I went back and forth to that outhouse from my bed so many times I must have worn a path into the ground. I knew I had a fever and my body was aching and, after the first few trips to the outhouse, all that was coming out of me was water. This went on all night long.

Finally, the next day I slept pretty well until early evening. When I awoke, I needed to go to the outhouse again. I walked into the front room, heading for the front door, and what I saw hit me like a ton of bricks. There was Debbie on her hands and knees with the English guy behind her and the Irish one standing in front of her; all of them naked and in the midst of an international threesome. They all glanced over at me as I opened the door to head to the outhouse.

When I came back, the guys were getting dressed and ready to leave. They mumbled some kind of unintelligible half-baked apology as they left. Debbie brought me some water and Lomotil to help get me through the night. I always had Lomotil around and knew it would immediately stop any type of stomach problem. I'd discovered it in East Africa the year before.

The next day, I told Debbie, "I'm leaving tonight. I'm heading back to Singapore to get the shirts ready for shipping back home and then I'm heading to Jogjakarta. You owe me money for your share of the fabric and to have the shirts made." She hadn't paid her share of money yet since she was mainly strung out on painkillers. "Send the money you owe me to poste restante in the post office there."

Debbie only had traveler's checks and I wouldn't have time for her to cash them before I left that evening. That night when I got dressed, I noticed my clothes were very, very loose on me. I took the ferry to Butterworth and then got the midnight train to Singapore. On the train, I took some valium and the next thing I knew, a guy was shaking me. It was morning, with light pouring into the train and a Malaysian border immigration officer asking me for my passport. He examined it and told me to gather my stuff and go with him.

I got off the train and walked with my daypack to an office just a few yards this side of the fence where Singapore started. We sat in that office all day. One guy after the next grilled me on why I was still in their country when my visa had run out two days earlier. Finally, late in the afternoon, they felt sorry for my emaciated-looking state and let me board a train from the border into Singapore.

I stayed at Peony Mansions, a travelers' hostel where I made some great new friends. A German, Detlef, was one I got really close to. We did all kinds of fun stuff for the next couple of weeks, playing frisbee soccer in the park in sunny weather and during thunderstorms, and often going to Chinatown to look for old treasures for bargain prices. I found a great piece of a Mandarin robe from the Ming dynasty which I still have. I had it framed in 1975 in San Francisco and recently took apart the beautiful frame and brought it back with me to Sihanoukville, Cambodia, where I now live.

Detlef and I went on day hikes around Singapore, outside the city and along the coast. We spent tons of time at the Orchard Road car parking facility where there were hundreds of stalls of every type of Asian food imaginable once the office workers went home each day and all day at weekends. Many evenings, we went out with some of the ladies who stayed in our hostel and partied.

I had to wait for the shirts to be finished and then ship them, then I'd be free to head down to Indonesia. The one thing that really stands out in my mind about Peony Mansions was the shower. The pipe with the showerhead attached that came out of the wall had an area around it that was totally open; maybe two inches of space all the way around the pipe.

Every time I turned on the water, a half dozen or more flying cockroaches would come out from behind the wall and fly around in the falling water, banging into me and the walls continuously while I was soaping up and rinsing off. It made me sweat, it was so unsettling. They were three inches long at least. This was *not* a luxurious place.

One night, Detlef said, "We should go down to Bugis Street for the open-air market." Bugis Street was named after the Bugis sailing cargo ships and their pirate crews that plied the waters of the South China Seas. They struck fear into many and the British later coined the term "Boogie Man" which was a reference to those pirates.

"They have a tradition that, at midnight on Saturday nights, they clear all the stalls off the intersection and the transvestites come out and perform."

"Well, Detlef, I'm up for that."

We went down there and out came the transvestites. After watching some really beautiful girls — uh, boys — playing instruments and singing, we were hungry so went down a side street where there were tables and chairs and people eating some great stir-fry noodle dishes. Before we sat down, I realized this wasn't one big restaurant but several. Every couple of rows of tables was owned by the guy on the sidewalk opposite those tables with a cart that had a couple of woks and he cooked all kinds of stir-fry dishes, both noodles and rice plates. At first glance, though, one would think it was just one restaurant.

The tables in the area closest to the intersection had more patrons than the ones further down the street. Detlef and I went down a few groups of tables, knowing that those were owned by a guy who wasn't getting any business as of yet. All of a sudden, a bunch of American sailors started showing up. The USS *Constitution* was in port.

Three of them sat down at the first restaurant and I yelled over to them, "Hey, why not come down here and give this guy," (I pointed over at the guy on the sidewalk), "some business?"

They got up from their table and walked down to where I was, choosing a table where I'd beckoned them to. Now everyone was happy except the huge Chinese guy who owned the restaurant near the intersection and where those sailors had been sitting until I yelled over at them. He walked quickly toward me.

"You stole my business," he said as I saw the fist coming straight at my nose. I quickly turned my head to the side and he caught me square on the jawbone between my eye and ear. I went flying off my chair onto the ground. I was pretty stunned. The guy who hit me turned around and walked away. Detlef helped me back onto my chair. The pain was intense. When I put my finger to my cheek, I realized that the upper cheekbone felt really soft to the touch. I could easily push my finger into the hole where the bone broke.

I told Detlef, "I need to find a hospital emergency room. This is really hurting me." We headed for a taxi. "You're a pretty big guy," I said to him. "Did you ever think about jumping in and helping me?"

"Ken, it was a better thing to not do anything otherwise twenty Bruce Lees would come out of the woodwork and descend on our asses, doing way worse damage than that one punch you received."

I could see his point. These Germans are always so analytical. I should have been there with an Irishman.

We jumped into the taxi and I told the driver, "Take me to a hospital emergency room please."

The driver asked, "Why do you need to go to an emergency room?"

When I told him what happened, he suggested we get the police and go back and have the guy arrested.

"Uh, no thanks, I don't want to see that guy again and, anyway, it was my fault."

When we arrived at the hospital emergency room, we found a seat after filling out some paperwork. I was hurting but there were only two people in front of me so I figured I'd be helped pretty quickly. When one guy went with a nurse into the area where the ER doctors were, I started a little countdown, figuring one more and I was on deck.

Suddenly, there was a commotion and through the doors came some paramedics with a guy bleeding profusely on a stretcher. They put him on a gurney and I realized right then and there I wasn't getting closer to being helped but further away from any kind of relief. This went on time after time and finally, after about three hours, I got to see a doctor. He told me there wasn't much he could do for me that night, that I should go back the next morning to the oral surgery clinic downstairs, and he gave me a half dozen Demerol for the pain to get me through until the next day. I took two right away and, within twenty minutes, I was floating on cloud nine. How sweet that was.

The next day, I went to the clinic and the doctor told me he could surgically repair the broken jaw. He said, "I would initially shave that side of your head from the top down to the ear. Then I would go in and push the crushed bone outward, to where it was before that big punch."

I envisioned myself traveling among my peers with half a head of hair and a good-sized scar. "So, doc, if I don't have that procedure, when I get older, will my face look distorted and will I have a difficult time chewing food, years from now?"

He answered no to both questions and I immediately was relieved and told him to forget about the surgery. He gave me enough of the Demerol for another week and told me to only take liquids through a straw for that next week. I followed his orders as directed.

Wouldn't you know it though, the first day after the jaw got broken and I couldn't chew a thing, I found a Foremost dairy café that had the best-looking hamburgers I'd seen since leaving the States. It made my mouth water watching people eating those juicy burgers but I stuck with the juices and also had quite a few Foremost ice cream milkshakes which hit the spot in that hot and humid climate. They also helped me gain a little weight back after losing twenty pounds from my bout with dysentery in Batu Ferringhi, albeit very slowly.

When that week was over, I really missed the Demerol but I did eat plenty of hamburgers and more milkshakes. It had been a bit of a healing period for me.

My bungalow in Batu Ferringhi.

TO INDONESIA

After a couple of weeks, it was time to check in with the tailors who told me the shirts were finished. I paid about $7 each, adding the cost of the fabric and the tailor's fee. They packaged them nicely, individually in clear plastic and ready for shipping. They even sent them to a shipping company who would send them back to the States where I'd pick them up at customs in San Francisco when I finally returned. I was pretty stoked, knowing I had a product waiting for me back home that I could make some money with.

Now I was done with the business venture and, since Debbie had told me she'd send me the money that she owed me to poste restante in Jogjakarta, I figured out my plan to get there. I'd heard about a Pelni Lines ship that stopped at Tanjung Pinang, an island off Singapore, and continued to Jakarta in Java. It was the cheapest way to go. There was a ferry boat that took you to Tanjung Pinang, a couple of hours ride, and I found out the Pelni Lines ship would be there in two days. So, I had two days to kill.

It was evening when I got there, really hot and humid and pretty dirty. There was nothing special about it. I quickly got a cheap room and passed out. I woke up early and couldn't sleep anymore, mainly because of so many mosquitos buzzing my ears. It was too hot to pull the sheets up over my face to avoid them. So, I got dressed and went out walking along the waterfront, maybe a half hour before the sun was going to rise.

There were several groups of men standing around some kind of fires, busy with something. I kept walking, killing more time, and one thing that stood out about the place was that I kept seeing old Chevys. Strange to see them in such a remote place. I was cold and approached one group of men who looked like they had something cooking. Yes, they did. They had a very big pot and were constantly stirring its contents. Then one would spoon out a bowlful and pass it to each of the men who would sip from it gingerly since it was pretty hot.

They gave me a bowl with a spoon too. It was some kind of porridge with milk, sugar, and mung beans. Wow, did that hit the spot. Great start to the day. They didn't even want any money. Very nice. I started walking around, looking at the sights as this was the first time I'd seen the place in daylight. After a couple of hours, I found a little restaurant, had some breakfast, and afterwards walked and explored further. As I walked along the waterfront, a guy and two ladies were walking the same direction and were within earshot. We started talking and, right away, I remembered one of them from Peony Mansions — Marilyn, a Maltese lady who was living in Australia.

She introduced me to the couple with her, Blaine and Zelda, and we hit it off instantly. They were from New Jersey and had gotten married a few years before and gone on their honeymoon to Botswana, Africa, as members of Peace Corps. They did two years there and then started traveling up through India to Nepal and down to South-East Asia and then Indonesia. Blaine reminded me of Cat Stevens with his curly dark hair and beard. He was so much fun. Tons of energy. I mean, what would you expect from someone from New Jersey? He was really into the music of the '60s, as was I, and we became instant friends.

The four of us hung out for the next day until the ship to Jakarta came, one with mainly Sumatran refugees that were heading to islands further east. The deck below was where the majority of the Indonesian refugees were situated. They had all their belongings with them — bags, kids, and many had goats and chickens as well.

That first night on deck was pretty uncomfortable, not being able to lie down. It was dark out and I had my small cassette player so put in my Led Zeppelin tape. During the first song, one guy lit a cigarette which lit up the area close by and, to my surprise, about eight or nine Sumatran guys were all squeezed in real close and holding their thumbs up, indicating they liked the music. It turned out these guys were all part of the Sumatran martial arts team on their way to a competition in Java.

The next morning, my new friends and I went to the chief purser who we asked about the possibility of getting a cheap cabin for the rest of the ride to Jakarta. We got a third-class cabin with two sets of bunk beds and a sink. We hung out in the cabin for the better part of the day, smoking weed and listening to my *Son of Schmilsson* tape and laughing our heads off. Harry Nilsson's best album, I still love it to this day.

We took time out to go to the ship's bathroom where they had many sinks, toilets, and showers. It was an unreal scene. We opened the door and it was virtual chaos inside. Firstly, the door was about a foot above the floor so, when you stepped inside, you had to step down and there were at least six to eight inches of water sloshing about. There were little kids running around naked, men and women washing at the sinks, turds floating around in the water, and, to get to any of the facilities, you had to walk through that obviously filthy water. It was totally disgusting, to say the least.

We decided to not shower or use the toilets and just turned around and left. Soon, there was a knock on our door and the guy said if we wanted breakfast to please follow him. We went into a mess hall area where there were already maybe 40 or 50 Indonesian men and women and, as we walked in, they all looked up and stopped eating. A waiter brought each of us a plate with a one-square-inch piece of omelet, some rice, and some green water floating around with a strand or two of some green leafy vegetable. And a cup of tea. The other people in the room didn't move until we finished eating and got up to leave. Then they started in again.

We peered through a window in the door after leaving and noticed they were all eating with their right hand. No utensils. In many places, as you possibly already know, the people eat with their right hand and wipe their butts with their left. That explains why the royalty in those places let the finger nails of their left hand grow very long, sometimes up to twenty inches or more. It signifies someone who has another to wipe their ass for them. Anyway, that was a pretty interesting trip. My first exposure to travel by sea in Indonesia. Not to be my last.

On the Pelni Lines ship from Tanjung Pinang to Jakarta.

JOGJAKARTA

Now I had a couple of new friends. We got off the boat in Jakarta and immediately had a run-in — well, Zelda had a run-in — with the customs guys as we checked into Indonesia officially. One went through her backpack and pulled out, of all things, one of her tampons. He stood there examining it, holding it up to the light, gently squeezing it before finally unraveling the fabric, trying to possibly spot some kind of weapon or stash of drugs, I really don't know. We all exchanged silly looks while he did his thing and finally he waved us through.

As we walked around in Jakarta, it struck us as a city of contrasts. There were some very modern, high-rise buildings and, right next door, were dozens of corrugated metal shacks with newspapers covering the openings that might be where a window would go in a more sophisticated dwelling. Many had cardboard rooftops and there were naked kids running around looking like they could use a good scrubbing. There was a narrow river going through part of the downtown and, on the banks, we could see dwellings made entirely of cardboard and newspaper. Women squatted down, washing stuff in the water. Right near them, we could often see one of those naked kids taking a dump. Just across the street were office buildings, hotels, and shanty towns squeezed together.

We got a hotel room and, early the next morning, took a train to Jogjakarta. Jogja, as it's commonly referred to, is one of the best-preserved and attractive cities in Java and is a major center for Javanese arts. It had many good cheap restaurants, inexpensive and comfortable budget lodging, and was a great place to learn about things like how batik is done as there were many classes to take to get hands-on experience.

Blaine and I took a class in batik. He was much more artistic and made a great batik T-shirt titled "Frenchman with joint." My best efforts weren't worth remembering. Blaine had the misfortune one day in class to accidentally knock over a container of boiling hot wax and it spilled onto his foot, which sent him jumping around in major fits of pain. He had himself a pretty bad burn and it took several weeks to heal up.

Blaine and Zelda had a pretty nice room in a more upscale hotel with beautiful gardens all around. I chose something more spartan. It was a former brothel named Bu Purwo and the whole place was made of bamboo. It had very small rooms, just large enough for a double bed to fit in, with bathrooms to share. These bamboo walls were very thin and you could easily hear the people in the rooms nearby.

In fact, there was an English couple — the girl was a gorgeous redhead — in the room just on the other side of the head of my bed. The head of their bed was on the other side of that thin wall. My pillow and their pillows couldn't have been more than six inches away from each other. It made life interesting for me because, on several nights while I was lying there, I would hear heavy breathing and then the sounds of two bodies having a go with each other. There were lots of moans, a few of them mine even, but I tried to keep them muffled, and then the English couple's bed would start banging into the wall. I think we all had orgasms at the same time on a couple of those nights. That's what I call really good neighbors. Neighbors like that are hard to come by.

It wasn't all love and kisses for that English couple though. I heard them arguing a lot. I think the guy wanted to leave but the girl was really enjoying it there. I didn't want them to leave either as they were making life more interesting for me. One day, I heard them talking about breaking up. She indicated she was fine with separating and intended to stay while he decided to go back to England. I imagined myself as her rebound fling.

Sure enough, the guy left and I saw the redhead in one of the many cafés around town and introduced myself. We had some tea and spent that night together but, wouldn't you know it, the guy came back the next day and they were gone. Just like that.

*****

Blaine and I found another passion together. I remembered seeing lots of people with puka shell necklaces everywhere we went. In fact, Debbie's sister and a couple of her friends used to make exotic necklaces, many of them with puka shells. I'd bought one from them that was all puka shells with one nice piece of turquoise in the middle. They made others with lots of turquoise as well as coral and, on occasion, an ivory bead or two.

So, one day I found a pretty fantastic string of ivory beads in a store in Jogja and I thought back to those puka shell necklaces and decided a necklace of ivory beads and a few other cool additions might really appeal to people back home who were into jewelry. Ivory. Elephants or seals. I wasn't putting two and two together. I wasn't at all in tune as of yet with the reality of the horrors of animals being poached for their body parts. I loved that ivory bead necklace. I put an African trade bead in the middle and wore it around, getting mostly positive comments from fellow travelers.

On another occasion, Blaine and I came across a taxidermy shop. In the window, we saw stuffed animals, including a mongoose intertwined with a cobra in feigned battle. That was a popular one they would sell. Even then, I couldn't imagine anyone wanting to put something like that on their coffee table or mantle. What I did notice though was a stuffed bird of prey.

"Do you have other birds that you will be stuffing to sell?" I asked the shop owner.

"I have a whole 55-gallon drum filled with these birds that I'll stuff when I get a request for one."

"I'd really like to see them if you're OK with showing them to me."

We walked into the room behind the shop, over to the barrel with the birds, and then opened it. The smell of the dead birds and whatever solution he had them floating in inside that drum was godawful. He pulled out a few and I noticed these birds had very long claws, most of them very sharp. The light bulb went off in my head that these claws, spaced between the ivory beads, might make for a very exotic-looking necklace. Something with either American Indian or African influence but really just a half-cocked creation in the end.

The owner said he'd sell me the claws for something like a dollar each. I bought a bunch, as did Blaine. Since it was my idea, I got first crack at the claws on the bigger birds. They looked like some kind of eagle. Blaine said he was going to use his on a puka shell necklace. The claws weren't ready for stringing onto a necklace so we found a jewelry shop that would put silver caps in them with a loop at the end so we could easily string them. I later found a shop that had other beads and semi-precious stones and found a couple of great pieces of Tibetan coral that I put in the middle of the necklace on either side of my piece of turquoise from the puka necklace. My masterpiece was complete.

*****

There were so many interesting things about Jogja. Each day, I'd go down to the post office to the poste restante window to ask about a letter from Debbie, hoping for more money. And each day, there would be no letter. On one occasion, a young man said to me as I came out of the post office, "Hello, where are you going?" After the first couple of times actually telling people where I was going, I realized they didn't want to know but were asking which country I was from. Everywhere I went in Indonesia it was the same. With their limited ability to speak English, that was what they came up with.

This young man, Budi, and I started talking. "Ken, how would you like a tour of the city and afterwards come with me to my family's house to have tea and cake?"

"I'd really love to, Budi. I have no transportation. Will you be taking me around on your motorbike?"

"Yes, get on and let's go."

It was very cool to have a guided tour from a really pleasant and upbeat local. He took me to many of the highlights of the city, places I never would have found on my own. Some were shops of cousins or good friends and I felt a little pressure to buy a few souvenirs but nothing really expensive. Then he took me to his home where I met his mother and younger siblings. Nothing but smiles from everyone the whole time. They were so hospitable, bringing me a sweet cake and multiple cups of tea.

Budi asked me if I'd like to see even more of the city. I said sure so again I got onto the back of his motorbike and away we went. He took me all over town, to museums and schools and then to major high-end art galleries. He knew every artist in town and I think he took me to meet all of them to see their works of art. I ended up buying a couple of Cirebon cloud paintings, a style of batik. Cirebon is a city on the northern side of Java. I felt by purchasing a couple of batiks this friendly kid would see his day as being worthwhile in the end. I'm sure he got commission for bringing people to any art dealer if they ended up buying something. So, even if the hospitality was just a precursor for making a little money, it was the best way I've ever experienced to go shopping and see a city.

*****

Blaine and I regularly played with my frisbee. We'd go to streets that seemed fairly deserted and one of us would stand on a sidewalk with the other across the street on the opposite sidewalk. If a car came, we'd wait until it passed. Passersby would stop and watch us out of curiosity and then continue on. One day, Blaine called me over because he heard something around a nearby building. We walked to a field behind it and out came about twenty boys who must have been in their mid-to-late teens, all in shorts and T-shirts. There was a volleyball court there and they started playing. These guys were fantastic.

After playing the game we knew, they shifted and started using their feet rather than their hands. It was amazing how long they could keep the ball going back and forth; very entertaining, to say the least. Blaine and I were so inspired by these guys we went around the corner to Jalan Malioboro, a main street, where we were able to throw the frisbee across a much larger distance. We did so for a few minutes and then, when we had to keep hesitating because of the constant traffic, we stopped and went back to hang out and smoke our late afternoon joint. Weed was easy to come by pretty much anywhere in Indonesia.

The next morning, the lady who ran my hotel/brothel called out to me that she had a letter for me. Could it be the money from Debbie? That would be too good to be true! No, it had some kind of official look to it. I opened it up and really couldn't understand the content so I asked a few people and finally someone told me it said I was to report to the police station that afternoon at 1 p.m.

It wasn't too far a walk and I got there with time to spare. The curiosity was killing me. What in the world would the police want with me? I handed over the letter to the guy at the front desk. They brought me into a room and a couple of police officers, wearing very starched uniforms, asked me to sit down. They began talking about complaints that were made and said I had a bomb I was throwing around Jalan Malioboro. Then it dawned on me they were talking about my frisbee. I immediately relaxed, knowing it was nothing serious, but one look at their faces and I was tense again. They didn't take it lightly.

They wanted to see that bomb.

"It's not a bomb," I told them. "It's a toy that Americans play with. A game."

They drove me up to my hotel for me to get it and then we went back to the police station. There was a long hallway there so I told one officer to stand there and I went to the other end and threw the frisbee to him. He lunged at it but missed as it skidded down the linoleum floor. I laughed and said, "See, it's just a game."

They took me into the room again then took out a knife and cut a small wedge out of the frisbee, saying they were going to send it to a lab and have it analyzed. They ruined my frisbee! They handed me the now defective toy and said I could go and, if I wanted to play with it, I was to stay away from busy streets. I threw it in their garbage can, telling them they'd ruined it and now they wouldn't have to worry about me playing with it anywhere. Assholes.

*****

Jogja was starting to get on my nerves but there were lots of good times still to be had. I was mainly just so upset about the police destroying my frisbee.

One day, we took a bus to the heart of Central Java to Borobudur, an amazing Mahayana Buddhist temple. On the way, I noticed how unused to the intense heat and humidity I was. I had on shorts and a tank top, my usual attire. The majority of the guys on the bus, Javans, were wearing full suits of clothes with jackets. I kept opening the windows and they would soon close them, saying it was too cold. I guess once you're acclimated you notice the difference of 90 degrees versus 95. Not me. It was all hot.

After many hours, we pulled into a clearing in the jungle and there was Borobudur. Built in the ninth century, it is an amazing structure of nine stacked platforms, six square and three circular, topped by a central dome. As I climbed higher and higher on this massive temple, I saw jungle below in every direction and mountains in the background. I later discovered it's the biggest Buddhist temple in the world and is decorated with an astonishing 504 Buddha statues.

Another day, we all took a bus to Prambanan, a ninth century Hindu temple. It wasn't as long a ride as it was to Borobudur which I was very happy about that because Prambanan wasn't nearly as impressive.

When we returned to Jogja, we heard there was to be a lunar eclipse. I went with Blaine and Zelda to some place on a hill where there were dozens of travelers from all over. It was one big party. We drank some beers and there was a ton of weed, with joints coming at us from every direction while we listened to *Dark Side of the Moon* again. I loved that album and never got tired of hearing any song from it.

We all sat around, waiting for the moon to disappear and then reappear. It took hours and I met a bunch of new people while waiting. Afterwards, we all walked back to town. A girl from South Africa just broke up laughing and started pointing at my toes, telling her friends to look at them. She said she'd never seen such long toes. I saw her again in a few different places, including Lake Toba, and she would always start laughing, every single time.

The day after the eclipse, I was in a café drinking some tea while it rained outside. There was a funny custom there when it rained. Many times, I'd see one of the local ladies standing in a dress, just under where the water ran off a roof above. She'd let the water soak her while she soaped up and took an impromptu bath. The temperature usually heated up pretty quickly after rain and she'd dry in no time.

On one occasion, I was having my tea when a tall, beautiful American lady sat down at my table and started a conversation like we'd known each other for years. Sometimes, you know right away when there's chemistry and I think we both felt it very quickly. After an hour or so, she said, "Ken, I'm still wet from the rain. The café's air conditioning is keeping my clothes damp and I'd like to go back to where I'm staying and change my clothes. Would you like to join me?"

Why would I refuse? We walked over to what turned out to be a dorm-type place with one room and probably twenty beds. I thought *I* was staying in a cheap place. This couldn't have cost more than 50 cents a night. There were people sitting and talking all over the room, mostly on their beds. I don't remember there being any chairs. This lady and I were still talking away and she took off her blouse, bra, and her skirt, still talking away. She was magnificent. Incredibly beautiful. She didn't hurry to put anything else back on.

My mind was racing. *Does she want me to make some kind of move?* I wondered. *There's other people sitting around the room but maybe she doesn't care*. I was thinking fast. *If she doesn't care, should I?* In the end, I didn't make a move. It was just too weird with a room lit by daylight to have sex so openly. I regretted it shortly after.

Once she started putting her clothes back on, her attitude changed slightly. I think she was testing me and I failed the test. I've failed tests in school in the past but this was the worst kind of failing. I mean, passing the test would have been pure joy. What was I thinking? Well, it was too late. She said she'd see me later at some place and I left.

When I saw her again soon after, she was with a guy from Chicago. Just like that. I was out. The guy she was with I had talked to the day before. He had just come back from living with Dyaks in Borneo. He said he was with a tribe, living in a long house with them for six months. He showed me his tattoos on the front of his shoulders. They were about six inches in diameter and, in the middle, was a kind of flower with an increasing-in-size circular maze going out from it.

He told me the Dyaks had this tattoo to hypnotize tigers they came upon in the wild. It kept them safe from being attacked. He said he asked to have the tattoos done just before he left so they held a ceremony where all the village elders sat and watched the process. He wasn't allowed to flinch or grimace in pain while the tattoos were being done. It took twelve hours, all the while being watched over by the village elders. He wore his tattoos with such pride and now that lady I blew it with was with him. And she really made me suffer because, when she saw me, she gave him the biggest tongue kiss imaginable and then turned to me and chuckled, as if to say, "You could've been on the other end of this."

That was it. I told Blaine and Zelda I was leaving. We'd been in Jogja for a month now and it was time for me to move on. They were heading to Bali so I went along with them. I'd loved my three months there earlier in the year and missed being there. We took a bus late at night, via Surabaya, and made it to the ferry and on to Bali. I'd had a Balinese girlfriend when I was there the first time, Kim, and one of my quests was to seek her out and see if we could pick up where we left off.

173

My *losmen* in Jogja, a former brothel. She and her sister, below, ran it.

My *losmen* in Jogja and one of the sisters who ran it.

Blaine outside our batik class, showing off his newest work of art.

My batiks were so poor, I refused to hold them up.

Waiting for bus to Borobudur to leave.

Bus ticket.

TO SUMATRA

Once Blaine, Zelda, and I arrived in Bali, I took them to stay at the same *losmen* I'd stayed in earlier that year. Ahhh, nothing like the familiar feeling of Kuta Beach. I was excited to get back there but something I found on my return is the best part of travel is the feeling of awe one gets in a newly discovered place. I felt like everything was too familiar. Been there, done that, so to speak. Kim didn't even give me the time of day when I saw her again. Blaine and Zelda were loving this place, being there for the first time, but, after a week and a couple of those old magic mushroom trips at sunset, I longed for a new discovery.

Just like that, I told them, "You guys, it's been great being with you the last couple of months but I'll probably head up to Lake Toba, Sumatra, and Samosir Island in the middle of Lake Toba. I've heard some great stories about the place. So, maybe someday I'll see you there."

Lake Toba is the largest caldera in the world. A caldera is when a volcano, or a few volcanos, erupts and the earth drops out and fills with water. The Toba caldera was the largest volcanic explosion on the planet in the last 25 million years. The lake, which is set down in a crater, is nearly 19 by 62 miles. In the lake is Samosir Island which is inhabited by a tribe called Bataks. They had a history of ritual cannibalism, performed in order to strengthen the eater's *tendi*, or "life-soul." In particular, the blood, heart, palms, and soles of the feet were seen as rich in *tendi*.

Marco Polo wrote about the ritual cannibalism after he stayed on the east coast of Sumatra in 1292 for a number of months. He learned of the rituals from hill folk who told him about a condemned man who was eaten. It was alleged they suffocated him then had him cooked, after which his kin ate him, sucking the bones until not even a particle of marrow remained in them. The dead man's bones were then collected and put in chests which were placed in caves among the mountains where nothing could reach them. It was said that, if the locals took a foreigner as prisoner and he couldn't pay a ransom, they killed him and ate him immediately.

I headed back to Surabaya before taking the train to Jakarta. Just for a lark, while waiting for the train, I went into a pharmacy as I loved discovering how loose pharmacies around the world were. I ended up coming out with about twenty tablets that were some kind of stimulant. I didn't know exactly what they were — small flat round pills with a cross. I took a couple and had a coffee to enhance then and I buzzed throughout the train ride which took all day. After a few hours, it was an annoying feeling, not a good high, and no way I could sleep. I tossed the rest out the window.

The next morning, I woke up in my decidedly budget hotel and went down to the harbor in Jakarta where there were many cargo ships lined up. I went into the shipping office and they told me which cargo ship was going to Medan, Sumatra. Medan was the capital and a five-day cruise up the Straits of Malacca, the body of water between the Malay Peninsula and North Sumatra. This 550-mile long body of water has been famous for hundreds of years for the pirate activity that took place there.

I bought myself a deck-class ticket and purchased some snacks to take along with me, including a couple of kilos of boiled whole peanuts. I also had a new frisbee with me that I bought in Bali before I left and it came in handy on that cruise.

The ship set out that afternoon and I found that a huge portion of the deck had stacks and stacks of tires that were to be delivered to Medan. On top of sheets of plywood over the tires were four soft-top Land Rovers. I got comfortable on some of the tires, took off my shirt, and enjoyed getting some rays and meeting some fellow budget travelers. The not-so-budget travelers on the cargo ships had actual cabins but that was out of the question for me.

I sat next to some guy from Australia and we told travel stories, passing a joint back and forth as we looked over the rolling waves, listening to *Scheherazade*, the symphony about Sinbad and the sea. After a few hours, the sun was just beginning to set and, in the distance, maybe twenty miles away, was Singapore and the beginning of the Malay Peninsula. There were clouds above the land mass and we noticed flashes of light above the clouds. Periodically, maybe every minute, there would be a flash of light.

It became more obvious what we were seeing as the sun went down. As it got darker, those flashes became more defined and what was happening was an electrical storm; the flashes were bolts of lightning going in all different directions, mostly above the clouds. And not one of those bolts was the same pattern as the one before. Sometimes, it was straight for a distance and then it would tail off into something resembling a corkscrew pattern. This show went on for several hours until we could hardly keep our eyes open, wanting to just curl up and go to sleep.

In the midst of it all, we saw a line form on the deck. They were serving the evening meal but you had to have your own plate and utensils. I had none; par for the course for me. I was rarely prepared for any situation and inevitably would have to wing it. But I did have my frisbee. Voilà, a plate. When I got closer to the guy spooning out the meal, I could see this wasn't much to get excited about. Rice and fish heads for all. The crew and the passengers who paid for cabins got the meat of the fish. We were fortunate enough though that they poured the green water the veggies were cooked in over the rice. Yes, the crew and paid passengers got the veggies. My frisbee worked like a charm. I have to admit I never really got that fish smell off it after those five days.

The first night, I looked around and almost everyone on deck, mostly Indonesians, was curled up sleeping on piles of tires and against the steel walls around the ship. It was impossible to get comfortable and then it started raining lightly and I had no rain gear. I noticed the Land Rovers again, walked over, and realized I could climb in through the opening in the soft top. I got inside and, although I was dry, it wasn't very comfortable to just sit there and try to sleep. I wanted somewhere horizontal so I put one foot on the driver's seat and the other over the steering wheel. Still not that good but I was able to put my back on the passenger seat with my head crammed against the door. It was futile to get even close to comfortable but this had to do and at least I ended up getting a few good hours of sleep. Just knowing I was avoiding getting soaked outside helped a little too.

The next morning, we got our ration of rice and fish heads again. I could see this was going to be a three-times-a-day event. In the late morning, I was taken by surprise. One of the officers of the ship came up to me and told me to follow him. He took me to the captain of the ship. The captain was very nice but informed me, "Mr. Liss, I've been getting a lot of complaints for showing favoritism to you for allowing you to sleep inside the Land Rover. Of course, you never asked me if you could and you went inside the car on your own but the locals in deck class are pretty upset about what they feel is special treatment by me. So, I have to ask you to please not sleep inside the cars anymore."

Damn, I thought I had a good thing going. We conversed a little more as he was interested in where I was from. That conversation helped out in a way too as a few of his fellow officers saw me with him, one being the head of the galley where the food was prepared. Once a day, he was kind enough to open the galley door onto the deck and wave me over when no one was around and he'd hand me a nice croquette, a ball of mashed potatoes deep fried. I felt like a puppy dog waiting around the galley door and then sitting up and wagging my tail when the door opened though instead of him tossing it into my mouth he'd just hand it to me.

By the end of the third day, all my snacks were gone and I was pretty hungry all the time. At night, I'd sleep on the plywood, under the Land Rovers since getting inside was a no-no. On a couple of heavy rainy nights,

181

it was only a matter of time until I got soaked, even though lying under the cars offered some protection.

On the morning of the fifth day, we stopped about 100 yards from the dock. Excitement was everywhere because of the anticipation of finally getting off this ship. An hour passed and then another and still we hadn't moved. People were packed up and getting restless, wanting to take that walk down the ramp to land. We were told we were second in line for an open berth but not when one would be available.

After a third hour passed, I was starting to think how desperately I needed to get off since I needed to get to the bus to Parapat, Lake Toba. In my *Lonely Planet* guide book, they said the last one left at noon each day. It was already around 10 a.m. I saw some fishing boats and small motor boats nearby. I went over to the edge with my daypacks and waved at the boats below, trying to get someone's attention. Finally, a motor boat came near and I asked the guy if he could take me to the dock. He said yes and I climbed over the side and down a rope hanging from the ship to the little boat.

The guy told me he could only take me to one of the ships tied up at the dock so I gave him a few rupiah and he took me to one that had a rope ladder hanging down. I climbed up onto that ship, walked across the deck, and down the ramp onto the dock. I was finally on land.

*****

It was 11 a.m. and I was running around the city of Medan, asking people for directions to the bus station for a ride to Lake Toba. I made it to the bus station and found the bus just minutes before it was about to depart. I was hot and sweaty and still really hungry. I saw many restaurants while I was searching for the bus station but didn't want to take the time to eat for fear of not getting on that bus. Once I'd made up my mind where I wanted to go, hunger wasn't going to stop me.

I sat down on the plywood seats at the back of the bus as all the seats in front of me were taken. It was weird but many of the passengers, all of which were locals, turned and smiled as they looked at where I sat down. I found out why soon enough. The seats in the back were right over the rear wheels and that was where the most of the shockwaves from the uneven road were absorbed. For five hours, I bounced up and down onto the plywood below me. At first, it was just uncomfortable with my adrenalin flowing in anticipation of being on my way to a great destination. After two or three hours, it evolved into straight-out pain and, for the last couple of hours of the ride, I sat there with tears flowing down my face. In a comfortable vehicle, the ride would have been great as we passed through

182

beautiful forest and rubber plantations.

Finally, we made it to the town of Parapat. It was late afternoon and the sun was going down. The lake was beautiful. I got off the bus and there was a small dock there where a boat with a sign on it saying Samosir Island was revving up its motors. I got on board along with a few locals. It was about seven miles across to the island and I noticed that, behind us, we were pulling three water buffalo. A rope had been tied from the back of the ferry boat to rings in the noses of the buffalos, with one just a few feet behind the other.

We stopped briefly at Tuk Tuk before continuing on to Tomok. I'd read Tomok was the least inhabited area as far as travelers went as most headed to Tuk Tuk with several hotels near the lake. In Tomok, the guide told me to just approach any home and ask the person living there if they had a room for me.

When I got off the boat, it was almost dark. Standing on the dirt road off the dock, a guy greeted me. An American guy. He was tall and thin and wearing a sarong with a button-down, short-sleeve shirt and a hat. His name was Seamus Magee and he was from Indianapolis.

"Hey, welcome to Tomok, friend," he greeted me. "Do you have a place to stay already in mind? If not, Mongoloi's place is right down here, about 100 yards away. I stay upstairs from the family and they have a great restaurant there too."

We walked down a small dirt path with the lake just to our right. We finally came to two thatched-roof buildings with rooftops that rose up on the ends. Both had entrances that faced the lake. We walked into an open-air restaurant on the ground floor with just four picnic-sized tables and benches. Mongoloi was in the back, preparing the night's dinner. Seamus introduced me and told Mongoloi I was going to be staying there. Mongoloi was all smiles. He was a stockily built guy with a handsome face and he was really charming and outgoing and spoke very good English. Having many travelers staying with him and eating at his restaurant helped him pick up the language fluently. The cost to stay there along with three meals a day was fifty cents.

I headed up some wooden steps to the first landing. That room was where Mongoloi and his family lived. Another flight of wooden steps up and we were in the top room, where Seamus was staying. It had a big rice mat covering most of the floor and maybe eight small mattresses, a couple of inches thick at most, strewn about. On three sides, the thatched roof came down to about 30 inches above the floor, leaving an opening with beautiful views on those sides. The view out to the lake and the cliffs in the distance beyond was spectacular. Above us was the high thatched roof. We sat down and Seamus rolled a joint. A perfect start to my stay.

On shrooms around sunset at Kuta Beach, Bali.

Me and my bird claw necklace. Blaine with his famous 'Frenchman with Joint' batik shirt. An American friend with us. We were all tripping on shrooms.

Blaine heading to the beach.

Trishaws, a main way of getting around Surabaya.

Typical South China Sea craft.

SAMOSIR ISLAND

Seamus had already been in Mongoloi's house for a couple of months. He was a former Marine and Navy Seal, having spent eighteen years in the Marines before training to become a Seal. He was one of the Seals who mined Haiphong Harbor in 1972. On the way back to his submarine, gunboats fired shots into the water and he got three bullets in his back. He'd had one of his teeth hollowed out and a tiny packet of an amphetamine placed in it and, after being hit, he bit down on it and instantly got enough energy to swim really fast back to the sub and get medical attention. He suffered from a temporary paralysis and was discharged and went back home to Los Angeles where he was confined to a wheelchair for a year, having all kinds of treatment and therapy.

One day, he and other wheelchair vets stormed into Senator Alan Cranston's office in Los Angeles and chained themselves together until the FBI showed up. The agents took Seamus aside and into a private room and said to him, "What do you want?" He said he'd been routinely turned down regarding a pension, which was typical of the Department of Veterans Affairs not buying into the possibility that a vet was actually injured in battle conditions. The FBI people offered to secure him a set number of dollars per month, starting immediately, with cost-of-living raises. Seamus agreed and promptly wheeled himself out of Cranston's office as the FBI guys tended to the other chained vets.

Several months later, Seamus was back on his feet again. He did a lot of musical theater in Los Angeles and was able to belt out song after song from a bunch of Broadway musicals. He was a pretty good Irish tenor with no fear. He'd sing for anyone who asked and many times even if nobody asked. He knew some plays so well, he could do all the dialogue, stage cues, and music.

We were constantly being visited in that room above Mongoloi's restaurant and family quarters by travelers who'd heard not only about Seamus' ability to entertain but also about our pretty fantastic library. We had several shelves full of books in that room. People who traveled a lot would have books they wanted to unload to lighten their packs or bags and we'd trade them two of theirs for one of ours. I don't know how Seamus came up with that formula but we had few, if any, raise much of a protest. Over the three months I was there, the book total grew and grew to over 300 books.

*****

As usual after a week almost anywhere new, I had constipation. New diets always have done that to me and moving from one area to another and being at the mercy of what food you can get your hands on was, and still is, an ongoing problem for my bodily functions. It takes time in a new place to find the right food that will do the job.

The smell of clove was a popular one in Indonesia. They have cigarettes called *kretek* that mix clove with tobacco and they give off a very distinct and pungent smell. One day, my curiosity got the better of me. I asked someone for one and lit it up. Two puffs later, my body came alive. I mean, it was like someone flicked a switch. Having very little time to think, I turned up the path that led toward the cliffs, in the opposite direction of the lake. I remembered there was the coolest little public bathroom on that path through the woods. There was a 30-inch-high bamboo square wall with a gate and, in the middle of the approximately 5 ft. by 5 ft. area, was a squat area with the hole in the ground. So, I went there, and quickly. So quick that I think, if there was someone with a stop watch, I might have set a world record for the 100-meter dash.

It is totally being one with nature when you're in the woods, with birds chirping in the trees above, and you squat down, do your business, and can watch people moving about around you. Privacy? Forgeddaboudit. But nobody really wants to come over and stare at you while you're at it. After that experience, I had a *kretek* every day and was a very happy camper. It took me a year after returning home from that trip to give up smoking.

Seamus, having been in Vietnam, had a peculiar habit, borne out of the fact that he had a lot of experience with night watch. His internal clock would allow him to sleep for 45 minutes and then he'd wake up, roll a joint, smoke it, and then go back to sleep for another 45 minutes. In the three months I was there, he never failed to do this routine. So, we always had some weed around.

One day, he announced that he was getting low. He'd heard there was someone selling pounds on Samosir Island and suggested we should buy one then sell some ounces to get our money back. In reality, it was so cheap that, even if we didn't sell any, we weren't out much financially at all. A guy came by and Seamus did the deal with him. He told us how his Aussie buddy got busted trying to ship many kilos out of Medan by ship and was arrested. He was in jail in Medan and, although he was incarcerated, they

190

didn't take the weed from him and visitors were able to buy it from him while he was in the slammer, with the authorities taking a small cut. It was funny how things worked over there.

We had all this weed but we needed some kind of baggies to break it up. In the little village near where the ferry boat dropped me off, there was a kiosk that sold what looked like puffed rice treats in small plastic bags. Seamus bought up about 40 of them and we took out the treats and put them aside as we bagged up the weed. Our problem now was what to do with the treats as we didn't want to throw them away. We knew the little kids enjoyed them a lot. I had an idea.

The next morning, Seamus and I went out really early so we could be on the road when the school children paraded by in their uniforms. They were from five to eight years old, very cute, and were led down the road with an adult in the front of the line and one in the back. As they marched by, Seamus and I handed each one of them a puffed rice treat. Their smiles were huge in anticipation as they walked toward us. It was the cutest thing and, in a matter of minutes, we had given all of the treats away.

We never sold one bag of weed. We were just giving it away mostly. And it wasn't really all that potent. For Seamus, it didn't matter. He just liked the hourly ritual of rolling a joint and smoking it. I remembered that, when I had bad weed back in San Francisco, I used to eat it and I could get really stoned out. I didn't need good stuff to have a major high.

I decided one day, feeling really frisky, that I would cook up something with the weed. I usually would heat up the stuff that I was using before putting it into brownie batter but that took an oven and we didn't have one. So, I made some pancake batter and threw in a bunch of the stuff and cooked it up. Then I put some jam on it and scarfed it down. That was in the evening.

The next morning, I woke up with horrible cramps, the kind that doubled me over and forced groans out of me. I was in my room and I guess Cass, the cook down in the restaurant, heard me. She came up and asked what was wrong and I told her the story about eating the weed the night before. She left and came back fifteen minutes later with a bowl of what looked like salad dressing. She pulled up my shirt and rubbed it around my stomach. She rubbed and rubbed and rubbed. After 30 minutes elapsed, I realized the pain had totally subsided. This lady knew what she was doing. Thank you, Cass. What a sweetheart.

Mongoloi's place.

Mongoloi and Kira and some old drunk who wandered into the picture.

Mongoloi's place from the lake.

Seamus reading one of many books we had up on our bookshelf.

Seamus with Mrs. Mongoloi and family.

Seamus charming the ladies. Penny second from left. On the left is Cass who worked there and helped me with my aching tummy.

Mongoloi's son helping himself in the restaurant.

Mongoloi's daughter takes a meal break.

MONGOLOI'S

After being at Mongoloi's for a while, I became part of the family and they'd let me use the kitchen whenever they weren't making a meal for a customer. I used to love cutting up potatoes really thin to make chips, deep frying them. There was a small market twice a week on the road to town, maybe 50 feet away from our house. One of the ladies who would show up always had avocados that were the size of softballs. Another had wonderful tortilla-sized tapioca chips which were crispy and so light. Each market day, I'd buy 50 of those tapioca chips and two or three avocados. In the kitchen, I'd use their wonderful mortar and pestle and grind up chilis, garlic, onions, and other spices, and then add to my chunky style avocado and chunks of tomato.

Some days, the mortar would already have a bunch of chili on it from the previous user and, after a few bites, our mouths would be so hot, we'd get up and bolt right into the lake and just drink the water as we swam. Then try again. Man, that was tops. In the afternoons on days when we had avocados but no tapioca lady, I'd make the potato chips to use with the guacamole.

Seamus and I were so much a part of the family that Mongoloi and his wife had us over to the house next door for a New Year's Eve dinner. We had lots of beer first while Mrs. Mongoloi, that's what we always called her, prepared the dinner. Out came the first course, a pâté of some sort, which was delicious. At Mongoloi's restaurant, it was fish every night with a variety of vegetable dishes, some with a peanut sauce, some curry, potato croquettes, etc. The pâté was the first thing, meat wise, we'd had for over a month.

After that was finished and we'd drunk more beer, Mrs. Mongoloi brought a savory curry, maybe goat, although they didn't have any goat that I remembered seeing. The Batak houses were built with the first floor of the house a good five feet above the ground, allowing them to store their animals underneath when necessary. The bottom was open-air too to allow for ventilation. So, it was possible I never saw a goat as it might have always been underneath.

The curry was served with plenty of rice and even more beer. It was a very festive night and Mongoloi told us about some of the history of Tomok. The next day, we woke up and went about our business but our usual friend, Fleas, Mongoloi's dog, was nowhere to be found. He was always following us around as soon as we came down those wooden steps, passing Mongoloi's room and down to the restaurant. After eating and a stroll around Tomok, we saw Mongoloi walking down the road toward us. He bid us good morning and told us he enjoyed having us for dinner to celebrate New Year.

"Mongoloi, we haven't seen Fleas around this morning. Have you seen him?"

"Fleas?" Mongoloi asked. "We had Fleas for dinner last night." Turns out Fleas' brain was the pâté and the curry was the rest of him. Burp.

*****

The women were very hard working. Most of every day, Mrs. Mongoloi would sit behind the kitchen and shell peanuts with Cass. On many days, I'd join them for an hour or so and just enjoy the sunshine and try a few words of Bahasa Indonesia with them but, mostly, we'd just enjoy the moment while shelling peanuts.

Mongoloi had a peanut farm along with raising the carp. Once the baskets were filled, Mrs. Mongoloi and Cass would haul the peanuts to some place down the road to sell. The first two months I was there, Mrs. Mongoloi was pregnant. One day, I asked Mongoloi, "Where's Mrs. Mongoloi this morning?"

"Oh, she began to have labor pains this morning so she went to the hospital."

"I haven't seen a hospital around here, Mongoloi."

"It's not around here, Ken; it's nine kilometers away. She walked there when the pain began."

"While she was in labor?"

"Yes, she's been through this before with our first two kids."

Late that afternoon, while shelling peanuts with Cass, I saw Mrs Mongoloi walking back with the baby in a sling on her chest. That was some day for her, I would say. Two days later, she was shelling peanuts again. What a trooper.

*****

As they didn't have books to tell their history, a historian was designated who could tell the history verbally when the occasion called for it.

Mongoloi's father was a village historian and passed all his knowledge down to Mongoloi who told us how missionaries used to come to Lake Toba and Samosir Island. They usually came with an entourage and would set up camp for a time. Then they would leave and, years later, the same type of scene took place, only for them to pick up and go.

At some point, a church was built but the presence of Westerners wasn't prominent, other than the long-haired, young, budget travelers who pretty much dominated. Just like anywhere else, if it's cheap, they will be there. Then he told us about the last missionaries to come. Turns out it was two guys from Boston. They were approaching Tomok and were still a few miles away and, when they were spotted, the runner hurried back to the tribe and told the chief about the two strangers approaching. The chief asked if they were with an entourage and the runner told him they were alone. The chief then told his people who gathered around to prepare them for dinner. The men arrived and, after a brief conversation with some of the tribe, the tribe members stripped them down, cooked them, and ate them. Mongoloi had a good laugh telling us this story.

He also told us they performed white magic on occasion for mostly positive purposes such as to bring on some rain or settle a dispute between neighbors to bring back the tranquility the dispute might have caused. In order for the white magic spell to be successful, there was a need for a type of dust that they could manufacture when they ran short. The chief would ask for a family to volunteer one of their children. The child was taken to a cave to be fed very well for a period of time, something like 30 to 40 days. Then the child was hung from his hands, dangling above a large container, and the bottom of the feet were cut open so the blood could drain out. They left the child hanging there for another prolonged period of time and, when they came back, the bodily fluids would have mixed with one another and dried in the container. That dry mass was then further processed until it became a powder they could easily scatter in their ceremonies. Offering up their child was an honor for the family.

Seamus was always such an entertainer. On numerous occasions, travelers from Tuk Tuk would show up and come up the wooden steps until just their head peaked into the room. They'd announce they'd heard about Seamus' stories and song and would he possibly like to try some of their weed or hash? A nice offering to gain entrance and have a fun afternoon.

I remember one guy from Michigan who came in. He had a guitar and, while he played pretty popular folk songs and light rock, more people showed up and it was like a glee club having a terrific singalong. He was really great. It would have been nice for him to stay there but people came and went quickly when on the road.

I remember another guy from the States who had long, flaming red hair and raggedy capes. He looked really worn out and pretty sick. We asked him what his story was and he said he'd been traveling for over a year and ran out of money several months ago. I asked, "How can you afford to keep traveling?"

"I just keeps moving and that pretty much takes care of everything," he told me. He left as fast as he came in, not seeing any free food in our room or offers to stay over, free of charge.

The best time ever for visitors was a day when we had a real full house. Seamus did *Cabaret* from beginning to end while everyone passed joints around and the room was thick with smoke. It was late afternoon and, out of nowhere, a French guy blurted out, "I can eat pussy better than anyone, anywhere." He said it a couple of times more and then an Australian girl got up and walked between the people lying on the floor, over to the French guy. She then sat down, leaned back, pulled up her sarong until she was bare from the waist down, and said to him, "Let's see what you got, Frenchy!"

The place went silent. He opened his shoulder bag and pulled out some chop sticks and proceeded to twist them between her thighs, getting her hair to wrap around them, and he opened her up. He then put his face down there and went to work. It was still silent as hell except for the sounds he was making and the beginning of her moaning.

Well, this was just too much for most of us to handle. A beautiful brunette pulled me over to her and we started making out and, although I wasn't paying too much attention to the rest of the crowd, I knew more people were pairing off and starting to partake in the carnal festivities. This went on for quite some time and I remember lying there naked with this girl, dozing off as the sunlight disappeared then us waking up, clinging to one another in candlelit darkness.

When we came to, the girl said to me, "What's your name?" We broke out laughing. And those who were still there all broke up laughing too. Everyone got dressed and we all went down to Mongoloi's for his smorgasbord dinner; 50 cents if you weren't staying there. I got to know this Aussie lady over dinner and saw her two more times before she took off for Bali. The opportunities that present themselves while traveling are rarely duplicated back home.

*****

One of the most amazing phenomenon while I was there was the weather as it was monsoon for the first two months. What that means in practical terms is most mornings were sunny and then clouds would move in in the early afternoons. At four p.m every day, it would start raining. You could set your watch to it. It would start raining and keep on going straight through the night and then clear up by daybreak. Every morning when you went outside, you would see the waterfalls pouring down the cliffs about a half mile away from the lake, behind our house.

The only variation would be whether or not it would rain hard right off the bat or start slowly and build up. Our preference, not that we got what we wanted very often, was for it to start slowly and build up. When that happened, the reeds that comprised the thatch roof would expand as the rain came down and little or no rain would come into the room. On the other hand, when it started like gangbusters, it would pour right through the reeds and it would be miserably wet inside until the reeds expanded. That could take up to five or more minutes and, by that time, we would be drenched.

The other issue was when the rain and wind came on fast. Having three open sides in the room with a 30-inch opening meant things went flying that weren't nailed down. It was a real comedy in there sometimes. For the windy times, Seamus had a bolt of fabric that was about ten yards long that could act as a sail, holding back the wind from destroying us inside the room.

Another thing I remember about the room were the inhabitants other than the travelers. The thatch roof, from just a few feet above the floor near the edges of the room and all the way up to the highest point, was the home to many, many spider webs. The webs and spiders down in the lower areas were much smaller than they were up high. The spiders down low, just above my head where I was sleeping, were about an inch and a half across, all black, and with yellow spots on the legs. Every morning, I'd see the spider come down and clean off the web. At night, there were always a lot of little flying things around the room and they'd get stuck in the web.

When the light of the day lit up the rooms, we'd see the spiders cleaning off the web and anything that moved was quickly wrapped in silk for a future snack. Once the web was cleaned off, they got right back up into the thatch. They never stayed in the web.

I liked to play with them so I'd break off a quarter inch of a matchstick and toss it gently into the web. The spider would appear on the edge of the web, coming down from its hiding place, and always go straight to the middle of the web and feel the vibrations of the object caught and immediately go over to that object, pull it off the web, then drop it, and go right back to its hiding place.

I didn't know how big the spiders were up high until, one sunny day, a bee, at least two inches long, flew in and went up near the top of the thatch roof. A couple of giant spiders came out of hiding and fought off the bee and we realized we were not alone! Holy crap, they were big.

Another thing I didn't realize was until one day someone was sitting in the room enjoying Seamus' singing and he pulled up the edge of the rice mat and, underneath, it was teaming with ants. We pulled the rice mat further back and then all over the room and there was no spot where there weren't hundreds or thousands of ants. Well, they never bothered us so why worry about them? We put the mat back where it was.

Walking past the cliffs of Samosir Island.

TOMOK AND LAKE TOBA

After I'd been on Samosir Island for about a month, Blaine and Zelda made their way up to Lake Toba and I found them one afternoon, sitting in Mongoloi's restaurant just after arriving. I was thrilled to see them. I was hoping they would stay at Mongoloi's but they'd gone to an area much further away from the lake and it was a real lengthy trek up to their house. So, during the time they were there, I only saw them a couple of times as they felt it was a long walk to Mongoloi's and wanted to go different directions than down to where I lived in order to explore the most of Danau Toba as possible. Danau is Bahasa Indonesia for "lake."

I loved the whole existence there and didn't miss the beach scene they'd just left behind in Bali. For them, however, it might have been too sedate. I think they were also getting low on cash so they headed out and, for the next few months, spent their time in Japan where, for a large portion of the time, they got jobs teaching English. For a high hourly wage, they would just speak English to a boardroom full of executives of large companies so they could practice their English. Blaine also found work doing commercials. He'd dyed his curly dark hair blonde and shaved his beard. He was living the life but mainly saving a lot.

I continued to enjoy the wonderful ambience of Tomok and Lake Toba. Every day, the farmers would plow their fields or rice paddies with water buffalo as their beasts of burden. At the end of each work day, little kids, five or six years old and totally naked, would walk the buffalo, held by a rope through the rings in their noses, along the path right in front of our house and down to the lake. The buffalo loved to swim. They'd lumber into the lake with these tiny brown-bodied kids on their backs and just float around. The kids would get up on their back, run a few steps, and dive into the water then they'd climb right back onto the buffalos and dive in again and again, having a totally exciting end to their day. When it finally got dark, they'd lead the buffalo out of the water and walk them back to their homes. What a sweet thing it was to watch.

*****

There was a young local kid, maybe thirteen or fourteen, who was always hanging around and just amazed by the look of the travelers. He came up to me one day and said, "Your moustache needs trimming." I had a pretty large one and the humidity made it very unruly most of the time. He found a shard of mirror, put it on a fence near our house, sat me down in front of that mirror, and proceeded to trim my moustache. Snip, snip, snip, he was just having a ball cutting it away.

He then brought the mirror closer and I looked in horror. He'd trimmed it down to what looked like a thin pencil line of a moustache. Inside, I knew I wasn't going anywhere, anytime soon, and it'd grow back but I still had to stop myself screaming. I was just blown away that my moustache was pretty much gone. The kid was really nice and I could see he didn't have much so I went upstairs and came down with a few T-shirts and a pair of shorts that fit him OK with a belt. He was so excited and I felt great doing something good for someone who really could use a helping hand.

The next day, the same kid walked up to me, along with a couple of his siblings and his mother. The mother handed me the garments I gave her son the day before. She told me, "You are interfering with the natural order of things. If you give all this to one child, you leave my other children feeling neglected and feeling sorry for themselves and jealous. This disturbs the harmony of our home. I cannot allow that to be destroyed, even if you think you are doing a nice thing so, unless you can give me things for all my children, I must give this back to you." She turned and left with her children. I was traveling light and didn't have enough to give them all equal amounts. So, I took the things back. It did teach me a lesson though about the pride of these people and how I had to respect that.

*****

Seamus had a monthly ritual of going to Parapat across the lake and getting a taxi to Berastagi, a town about 45 to 50 miles away. Berastagi had the nearest bank and he had his retirement money wired to it. So, the first two months I was there, I'd join him for the ride and then get out in front of the bank. Seamus would go in and get his money and, before we'd head back, he would treat the two of us to a steak dinner at his usual restaurant not far from the bank. We'd have a couple of beers and he'd order me a steak dinner and two steaks for himself. It was his monthly splurge since there wasn't much to spend money on in Lake Toba.

One incident that stands out was when, after leaving the bank one day, we passed a blind man who was sitting on the sidewalk. When he heard us coming, he held his cup up high in the air to get our attention. Seamus put a 1,000 rupiah note in, which was around $2.50. That was a much higher amount than most people would put in a beggar's cup; usually it would be more like a 100 Rupiah note or maybe two of them at most. The blind man made a mistake this time because he picked out the note Seamus put in, held it up to his face and said out loud in Bahasa, "1,000 rupiah, *terima kasih.*" Which means thank you. Seamus turned and pointed at him and started laughing, telling the guy, "You can see, you can see!" The fake blind man laughed along with him.

After a couple of months there, we had some new roommates join us, a couple of Aussie girls. Linda and Penny were both very cute; Linda a buxom brunette and Penny a buxom blonde. Within days, Seamus and Linda were an item. They did everything together. Penny was a lot of fun and, although we got close, it didn't lead to anything intimate.

After another couple of weeks, a third young lady, Kira, joined us. She was from England and also very cute and we really hit it off. After about three or four nights with the five of us sleeping in the same room, Kira, being very proactive, whispered to me, "OK, Ken, are we going to do it or not?" From that night on, Kira and I would put our mattresses together and cuddle and enjoy each other.

The five of us had all kinds of fun together. The girls instilled a different type of energy into that upstairs room. I was seeing a side of Seamus I hadn't seen before. He started to lose his earlier persona of an outgoing, very sociable guy and became more of a henpecked husband. Linda had him by the balls, no doubt about it. And he was glad to allow it. I was probably a little jealous, feeling like she came between me and my good friend of the last couple of months.

Penny, Kira, and I hung out and hiked over to Tuk Tuk and even took a boat around the island to some hot springs as the word was these were great. Hot springs never did it for me. There were little pools of scalding hot water to sit in and it was great if you liked sitting on jagged rocks while your ass was being burned to a crisp.

Penny had a terrific camera and one night, when we heard some thunder and lightning approach, she whipped out her little tripod and we went down to the restaurant where she attached the camera to the tripod. After the first couple of flashes of lightning, she set the shutter to open and left it for thirty minutes, saying she had experience in photographing lightning storms before. Sure enough, several weeks later, when we were in Penang, she took the film to be developed and brought back a large print of that exposure. It showed the lake in front of us fairly lit up, with the walls of the crater in the background, across the lake, and at least twenty bolts of lightning in the photograph, all different shapes and patterns. It was a really fantastic shot. One of those *National Geographic* cover shots.

Penny also had a cassette player and one cassette — *Bad Company*. We listened to that tape so often I could pretty much sing all those songs to myself, whether the cassette player was on or off. "Ready for love?" went through my head over and over again. When I hear that song now, it automatically transports me back to that house in Tomok. Not a bad thing.

The last and sixth person to move in was Suzanne who was in the Peace Corps in Korea. She had just finished a year there and was taking her 30-day trip to Indonesia and, ultimately, Lake Toba. She showed up just a few days before we were about to leave for Penang, Malaysia. Chinese New Year was approaching and we wanted to be there when the festivities began. Kira couldn't go as her travel time had run out. It was a bit of a tearful goodbye the day we all left for Medan. Suzanne was on board with going to Penang so, after taking the ferry boat in Tomok for the last time, the five of us took a taxi in Parapat, heading to Medan. It was really hard to leave. We had become such a part of Mongoloi's family.

From left: Penny, Blaine, Seamus in purple shirt, and Zelda to his left.

Zelda pausing before getting the ferry boat back to Parapat with Blaine.

The view from the ferry boat. I'm seeing Zelda off.

Kids playing with buffalo before going into the lake with them.

Daily ritual for the kids and the buffalo.

Batak kids who used to enjoy watching the crazy foreigners.

Seamus with Linda on the left and Penny.

PENANG

There were two ways to go to Penang. One was by ferry and the other was to fly. We heard the ferry was around a six- or seven-hour trip. Nobody was very enthusiastic about that so we splurged and got a one-way air ticket. We were lucky to arrive in Medan from Parapat in time to take the early evening flight to Penang. The five of us were all belted into our seats on the plane and sitting on the runway for what seemed to be an unusually long time when the pilot walked out of his compartment and told us a 55-gallon drum of paint had tipped over in the hold while being loaded. The top came off, creating a huge mess, so we would have to get off the plane temporarily. When we walked down the steps of the plane, there was blue paint dripping down the side of the plane and all over the runway below.

Back at the terminal, the Garuda Airlines people told us we would all be taken to a hotel where we would have rooms, food in the restaurants, and drinks anywhere, including the bars, all on the airline's dime, for as long as we had to wait for the flight out. Well, need I say this turned into a major party? We waited for eighteen hours until they came and collected us for the flight. We still had to wait a few hours at the airport until we took off but we were all pretty refreshed.

Arriving eventually in Penang, we immediately found a cheap hotel and decided the five of us would share a room. Having spent three months sleeping on a two-inch thick mattress on the floor in Mongoloi's house, we were prepared for any kind of temporary discomfort. After having a meal together, I wandered off on my own. I remembered how much I enjoyed opium when I was there with Debbie months ago.

I was walking up Chulia Street and it was pretty poorly lit. I felt a little intimidated until a Chinese man called over to me. "Hi, my friend, would you have any interest in smoking some opium?"

I walked over closer to him and said, "Where would we smoke it?"

He pointed to a small shack behind him. "I'm Jimmy Wong and I'm a retired insurance salesman. I come down here after dinner at home most nights and, if I see someone interesting, I invite them in to smoke some opium with me."

"OK, I'm interested in trying some."

He opened the door, which had a padlock on it, and we went in. Inside, he lit a Coleman lantern. The whole enclosure was no more than eight ft. by eight ft. The ceiling was low enough that you had to bend over when going in. The guy had posters of Jimmy Hendrix and Jim Morrison on the walls and, on the floor, were two rice mats with an opium lamp in between them. He also had two porcelain head stools with the angle on top that allowed you to rest your head comfortably lifted above the floor.

Jimmy was very knowledgeable about music that I was into and had a great boombox-sized cassette player playing familiar tunes in the background. While he prepared a pipe of opium, he told good stories. It was interesting to watch how the opium was prepared for smoking. He used a thin wire that he dipped into a small container of a gooey black liquid. Then he held the end of the wire, with the opium clinging to it, over the flame in the lamp. The liquid started bubbling and he immediately removed it from above the flame and rolled that mass of goo on the top of the bowl of the opium pipe. After rolling it, he again held it over the flame and, after more bubbling, he rolled it on the pipe. It was almost like a baker kneading dough.

Jimmy took a good two minutes working that gooey stuff until it became more of a solid ball which he put onto the hole in the bowl of the pipe. The pipe was about three inches in diameter across the top; very flat and made of wood. It was attached to an eighteen-inch length of bamboo. In the middle of the wooden bowl was the quarter-inch hole where he'd placed the ball of opium. Then he took the wire and moved it in the ball of opium in such a way that it spread the opium around the edge of the hole and partly protruding above the hole, looking like a small donut.

After all that preparation, Jimmy handed me the end of the bamboo and said to pull on it slowly and hold the smoke in. He placed the bowl upside down over the flame and let me do the rest. I was afraid I'd want to cough after continuously inhaling the smoke but I didn't have that sensation at all. Instead, I felt the smoke filling my lungs and I enjoyed the distinct smell of that burning opium, sort of sweet and pungent. After finally blowing it out, Jimmy prepared a pipe for himself. Then again one for me and we ended up having five pipes each. Turned out, each hit was about a half of a gram of opium.

By the time I had my third pipe, I wasn't really focusing on what Jimmy was saying but, instead, my mind was in the vivid dreams I was having while Jimmy's voice tailed off in the distance, mixing with the music. I felt like I was wrapped in warm blankets which provided me a bunch of colorful live action images. I was really enjoying the floating feeling again, just like many months ago in Penang, only better this time, without the presence of Debbie.

Eventually, Jimmy turned off the music and gave me a gentle shove, letting me know it was time for him to call it a night and return home. He was smoking a cigarette and, as I got up, I commented on how cool his cigarette holder was. It looked like shiny ivory but with dark brown streaks in it. He said it was actually polished bone and those streaks were from the tar in the tobacco. Then he put out the cigarette, tossed it to the ground, and handed me the holder as a gift.

I went back to the hotel to find Seamus and the girls and see if they'd like to go down to where the Chinese New Year celebrations were taking place. I opened the door and the room was lit with only one light bulb. Seamus was standing over a sink in the room and making those sounds you hear just before someone vomits. Sure enough, he puked his dinner right into that sink while the water washed it all down. One after another, the girls took their turn at the sink and each followed Seamus' act, with exact precision. I'd been floating on air and had come back to witness this? Very bad timing on my part.

My first thought was they'd all eaten bad food at the restaurant. Before I could ask Seamus if they had some kind of food poisoning, I noticed on a nearby table a bindle opened and white powder dust on the table next to it. After eating, they'd gone to buy some heroin while I was hanging with Jimmy Wong in his little opium shack. I felt like I had one-upped them, not getting sick like they did.

After about an hour, we went out to find the festivities. I noticed a couple of things right away. On people's front doors there were envelopes, sometimes five or ten of them. There were also long, thick incense sticks burning. These I found out were called joss sticks. I also discovered that the envelopes usually had money in them and were to settle debts incurred during the previous year.

We found New Year's revelers everywhere and the music in the streets was constant. Tons of fire crackers were going off and each and every one of those loud pops shook us to the core while we nodded at a café in the midst of it all. We spent a few hours trying to be part of the scene but mainly we were just five people struggling to keep our eyes open. It was a downright blurry night and one that convinced us to move on.

The next day, we moved out of Georgetown and up the coast to a village called Teluk Behang. We found a house for rent in a wonderfully placed location just a half block from the beach. Right across the street were five small houses in a row that were actually opium dens and a sixth at the end which was a doctor's office. I later found out that the doctor would give people injections of morphine or heroin, depending on their preference. I never did check that place out but the opium dens I knew like the back of my hand by the time I left Penang.

If the idea of living across the street from a bunch of opium dens wasn't wild enough, the island's main police station was a half block down on the same side of the street that our house was on. They allowed the opium dens to stay open as long as the owners of these dens paid the equivalent of $10 per month per lamp they had in their dens. The more lamps that were lit, the more business the dens were doing, was the assumption made by the police. It worked for them and was heaven for me.

TELUK BEHANG TO BANGKOK

We settled into our house with Seamus and Linda taking the upstairs bedroom and me, Penny, and Suzanne sharing the downstairs one. We figured the best way to share it was push the two beds together and the three of us sleep together. We all went to a market to buy some supplies for the house and Seamus cooked us some great veggie omelets with steamed rice.

That evening, I went out exploring, right across the street to one of the opium dens. It was nothing like Jimmy Wong's little shack. This place was a good-sized room with several rice mats on the floor and some Asian music playing at a low volume. There was already one customer being tended to so I lay down and rested my head on the porcelain head stool and waited for someone to come prepare me some pipes. It didn't take long and, six pipes later, I was off into dreamland. The opium was going for about 33 cents per pipe. Wow! Later I would find out that was fairly expensive but I was happy as a clam at that point in time. I was allowed to lie there for a couple of hours.

Eventually, I figured I might as well be in my bed as it was an easy walk back across the street. The house was pretty quiet when I returned. I heard Seamus and Linda upstairs but didn't hear or see any sign of the other girls. I lay down on my bed and enjoyed the nod and a new set of dreams while listening to The Velvet Underground's "Heroin" and "I'm Waiting for the Man."

Some time later, I felt movement on the bed. There was lots of heavy breathing. I didn't have to even suspend my dream to figure out it was my bed partners having a go with one another. Then I heard Suzanne say to Penny, "Wow, that was the best sex I've had in a long time. I'm going to get a coke in the kitchen. Do you want anything?" and she left the room.

"Penny," I said, "it sounded like you two were having a lot of fun." She rolled over, looking very tasty resting on her side with that long blonde hair and her breasts staring me in the face. Well, maybe I was doing the staring.

"Ken, you *heard* us? You looked like you were sleeping. Would you like to join in?"

I didn't even answer but reached over and gently pulled her toward me. While we were kissing, Suzanne walked back into the room and was aghast

225

at seeing us making out. She burst into tears and made it clear she wanted Penny for herself. I backed off Penny and let Suzanne know it was all right with me. Hey, I wasn't going to be very effective in any kind of love making while under the influence of opium so it wasn't a big sacrifice, even though just making out with Penny was damn good. What a doll she was and if I'd known she was into me that way back in Lake Toba, it would have been a different story. I was pretty much straight as an arrow there and ready to go at all times. Suzanne calmed down and, from that night on, she didn't view me as a threat so we could all enjoy each other.

It was an amazing friendship the three of us had. We'd go to the beach, go out to eat and even to the opium dens together. The girls didn't smoke the opium but would sit near me while I was smoking and, when I was done and in my dreamworld, they would wave their hand fans over my face to cool me and even whisper to me as they fed me small bites of fruit, warning me first, so I knew that they were putting something into my mouth. I'd chew on something they put in there, very slowly, and thankfully I never choked on anything.

Everywhere we went, I would walk between them, all three of us arm in arm. We were totally inseparable. Well, except when they were getting it on, but I would lie there right next to them while they were ravishing one another, both in the evenings and in the mornings too. It was always a great show and beat looking at porn magazines by a mile.

After a couple of weeks of this, my visa ran out and it was time to go. I took the ferryboat to Butterworth, on the mainland, where I could get a train. I was heading to Bangkok and had a couple of hours to kill before the train, coming up from Singapore, would pull in.

All of a sudden, I looked up and saw Blaine and Zelda. I barely even recognized Blaine. He'd shaved his beard and cut off a lot of the long curly dark hair and now had it short and blonde. On top of that he wasn't wearing his usual shorts and T-shirt but a very strange-looking powder-blue, polyester leisure suit. He reminded me of an old retired New Yorker who had moved to Miami Beach and was about to attend a party at the Kiwanis club annual stone crab fest.

They said they'd just come from Kuala Lumpur after a few days in Singapore following their time in Japan. They were also going to Bangkok. We boarded the train and sat in the second-class seats. It was a long ride and not very comfortable. After a few hours, who should walk into the compartment but Suzanne, who hadn't been around when I packed up and left. It turned out she had to leave the same day to get back to her Peace Corps gig in Korea. She came up to me while I was trying unsuccessfully to get comfy in my seat and have a good sleep.

"Hey," she said while she shook me a little, "I have a first-class sleeper car and, if you'd like to, you could join me in my bed."

"Really?"

I was trying to figure out if she was just being thoughtful and a good friend or if she wanted something more. But what a sweetheart for even offering. I went back to her compartment. There were just two berths and hers was the one on top. I got undressed and climbed in with her. Immediately she was all over me. This took me totally by surprise.

"I thought you were gay, Suzanne."

She said "I'm mostly into women but after all the time we spent together, I got a bit of a crush on you, Kenny."

This was knocking me for a loop after how she carried on when she found me making out with Penny a couple of weeks earlier. I started making out with her and soon realized I couldn't do it. Something inside me was telling me no. She really got pissed off at me. She read me the riot act and threw me out of her berth. I had many mixed emotions but the most prominent one was I'd had a chance to have a bed to sleep in and, all of a sudden, I had to go back to those lousy second-class seats with Blaine and Zelda.

After a long uncomfortable ride to Bangkok, we got a taxi from the train station to the Malaysia Hotel. All three of us took a room together there, trying to save our money for later on when we headed up to Laos. At this time, the Malaysia was a hotbed for budget travelers. This hotel was a dream. Each floor had its own room-service agent. You could call him at any time of the day or night and ask for almost anything.

I called him. "Hi, this is room 311 and I'd like some Thai stick." Thai stick was the best and most potent weed in the world at that time.

He responded, "How many do you want and which kind? The brown stuff or the light green, which is a bit stronger?"

An hour later, he knocked at my door with what I requested and the prices were amazingly cheap. Another time, when Blaine and Zelda went sightseeing, I knew I had the room to myself and I called the room service guy. "Could you bring me a call girl, a nice tall skinny one please?"

Thirty minutes went by and there was a knock at the door and, sure enough, it was a beautiful tall lady with hair down to her butt, my friend for the next couple of hours. This was an extravagance for me but I had to do it once, just for the fun of it.

The rooms were very plain and nothing to write home about but you did have your own bathroom and a ceiling fan and my new friend and I had a shower to begin our tryst.

Later that day, I remembered to give Andy a call, the Canadian Peace Corps guy I got to know in Bali. He said for me to meet him on a street called Patpong Road around 8 p.m. Blaine and Zelda were always good at doing their own thing and I didn't want to tag along all the time. Andy suggested a particular bar and, when I went in there, he was sitting in a booth with two females that he introduced to me as girls that worked the bar. It was their job to get customers to buy them drinks. The bar wouldn't put any real amount of booze in their drinks so they were making a good profit every time you bought a drink for the girls.

Most guys were easy marks for these girls. They were all very pretty and dressed very sexily. They'd sit really close to you, kiss you on the neck and cheek, and put their hands on you and even take your hands and guide them to some of their nice places. Not only were you ready to buy them drinks but many times you just wanted to take them back to your room or to a hotel for a "short time."

Andy and I were in no hurry so we sat with these young ladies and had several rounds of drinks, really taking our time, just enjoying these ladies. It was exactly what the average guy would hope going to a bar back home would be like but, knowing what the reality was at those bars back home, it was much, much better on Patpong Road.

Later, after paying what they called the "bar fine" to take the ladies out of their work, we took them to a hotel room where the four of us got down to business. Afterwards, we all took showers and then switched ladies and had another go. Around 2 a.m., the girls decided they were very hungry. They led us up a street, not far from the hotel, to a few carts on a sidewalk where people were making rice or noodle dishes with either veggies, meat, or both, with or without one of the many Thai curries. How nice it was to sit and eat delicious food outdoors until 3:30 in the morning on the streets of Bangkok with lovely young members of the opposite sex.

As I was saying goodbye to Andy, he gave me the phone number of his friend, Linda, his friend in the Peace Corps, who I also met in Bali. "Call her, Ken. She'd love to see you."

*****

Bangkok was many things, good and bad. The bad was the intense heat and humidity. It was pretty draining to be out and about and there was usually a ton of traffic so getting anywhere that was too far to walk was a real pain in the butt. There were motorized rickshaws called tuk tuks which made a lot of noise and were usually pretty cramped. So, wherever you went in one of these things, it was noisy, cramped, and you were breathing a whole lot of exhaust fumes. The city was full of pollution.

On the plus side were some of the really amazing sights like the wats, (temples), that were around the city, the food, the shopping, and the Chao Phraya River, which runs through Bangkok and the middle of the country. Bangkok is a great place to get around by boat too on the never-ending *klongs*, or canals. There are many festivals on or near the river and beautiful temples near the river such as Wat Arun, one of Thailand's best-known landmarks.

More fun on the water was at one of the floating markets, my favorite being in Ratchaburi. You had to drive out from Bangkok then stop in a beautiful countryside area, park your car, and get onto a boat in a canal nearby. Traveling along the canal, you'd see dozens and dozens of boats which were selling everything imaginable. You could pull up next to a boat and the proprietor would make you bowls of noodle soup with wonderful chicken broth and you'd eat it right on the boat. I was a little suspicious when they washed the bowl out in the river after we handed it back to them. I never did get sick from the floating-market food though.

In the hotel lobby of the Malaysia Hotel, I ran into another friend I made in Bali — Bruce, from Newport, Rhode Island. He said he'd just pulled into Bangkok that day and got a room at a hostel. Bruce lived even more cheaply than I did. First, he asked me if I had the key to my room and, when I said yes, he asked if we could go there. He had a bunch of Thai stick and wanted to make it more compact for when he went back to the States with it.

In my room, he took out some 35mm film plastic canisters. Then he started breaking up some weed he'd purchased and began packing it into them. He put the bottom of the iron bedpost leg into the plastic canister to press the weed down to become really compact. Then he'd repeat the process. He was able to get 25 sticks into one canister and did the same thing with another canister too. He said he'd carry those two through customs along with 30 other canisters that had film in them, all in his camera bag, and skate right through customs.

I found out six months later, talking to him on the phone, that, when he came through customs, the agent opened both of them in the first ten he checked. Then he looked at Bruce, put his finger up to his lips, and indicated shhh. He told Bruce to go into a side room with him. "If those two canisters are all you have with you, I'll let you leave but, if you have any more than those first two, I'm arresting you right here and now. I'm gonna do a full body search on you so take off your clothes and bend over."

After he did a full cavity search and checked the rest of Bruce's film canisters and other bags Bruce had with him, he waived him on his way. Good thing he didn't take three of them...

Anyway, back to the room. When Bruce finished his chore, he and I decided to check out the same bar I'd been to with Andy a couple of nights before. We sat down in the booth and again immensely enjoyed the goings-

229

on. There was a stage with dancers and one really tall beautiful girl on the end of the stage near us kept smiling toward us. She was the spitting image of Juliet Prowse, a famous dancer from Fred Astaire movies. Long beautiful legs and gorgeous face. I got up and went closer to the stage and started gesturing to her to see if she'd like to come down and talk with us.

Right away she got down and approached us and I knew immediately I wanted to be with her. Bruce also intimated he was smitten with her and I asked if he'd like to split the cost and we'd go have some fun with her together. We paid the bar fine and she left with us. While we were walking down the street, she started talking to us about what we were going to pay her. Before I could answer, we were in front of our hotel and Blaine and Zelda were just coming down from the room. I told them our situation and asked if it was OK if Bruce and I took the girl up to the room and had some fun. Blaine was totally OK with it but Zelda was very obstinate about us not going in there under any circumstances with that girl.

Bruce, the girl, and I started walking again and we asked her if she knew of a good hotel room for a couple of hours. She suggested a place and, when we reached the reception area of this pretty dingy place, she started talking about her fee again. We started adding it up. Bar fine, her fee, room cost, and Bruce balked.

"I can't afford all this money, Ken. You're on your own. Sorry."

Well, this was now way too much for me to afford alone. "I'm very sorry," I told her, "but, giving it second thought, we don't want to go any further with you tonight."

We started walking back to Patpong Road and the whole way this little piece of heaven turned into the Wicked Witch of the North, giving us real nasty attitude and foul language until we turned onto Patpong. She then sped up when she saw some friends of hers on Harley Davidson choppers in front of the bar. She turned and pointed toward us while talking very loudly and looking visibly upset. Bruce and I took off running in the opposite direction and made it back to the lobby of the Malaysia Hotel and disappeared upstairs away from any potential violence directed toward us.

I don't even know if those bikers followed us at all but the girl was very angry that we took her out of her night's work and now she would be without tips for the rest of that night and no money from *farangs* for *boomsing. Farang* is what Thai people call foreigners. *Boomsing* is slang for having sex.

Blaine, Zelda, and I left the following morning on a bus to Nong Khai on Thailand's northern border which is right on the Mekong River. From there we got a ferry to Vientiane, Laos.

VIENTIANE

We took the boat across the Mekong and went through customs in Vientiane, which turned out to be an opium eater's triple-E ride in Disneyland. We found Saylom Villa, a bit of a run-down French colonial mansion that had a variety of rooms, all dirt cheap. It was near an equally run-down Vietnamese refugee encampment a half block away.

Right next door was a house with a sign saying, "Cold sweet yoghurt here." That turned out to be a daily destination. Saylom Villa was so inexpensive, I didn't even bother to ask Blaine and Zelda to share a room; I got my own. It was 45 cents a day and that included maid service and also the washing and folding of your clothes.

First thing we did was go down to the marketplace and browse. There were all kinds of goods and arts and crafts but what hit me so hard were the women sitting behind huge bales of marijuana, rolling joints. They were rolling big bombers and they'd put a rubber band around fifteen of them and sell the bunch for ten cents.

I was thinking, *Why bother selling it at all if it's so cheap?*

Travelers lazily strolled down the streets while smoking the joints and even walked into shops with them still lit. Nobody seemed to care. This was at a time when the Pathet Lao soldiers were slowly working their way into Vientiane, getting ready to take control of the government in a bloodless takeover. There were already Pathet Lao soldiers there and their compound was right across from the market. On occasion, I'd even asked one of them if they had a light and he pulled out some matches and lit my joint for me. They were pretty young guys and always smiling.

The market where we bought the weed also had cheap breakfasts we enjoyed quite often. Chapati was always the main choice with some hot tea.

The first evening we were staying in Vientiane, I went exploring near the villa and, just a couple of minutes away, there was a ramshackle group of houses where, to my delight, I detected the pungent smell of opium mixing with a variety of spices wafting through the air. I went into my "all alert" mode and easily discovered the house it was coming from. The door was open.

I peered into a nearby room and saw the rice mats on the floor, one of which was occupied by someone taking a long pull on his bamboo pipe. After a moment or two, he picked his head up off the porcelain head stool and looked over at me and asked if I would like to partake? Does a bear shit in the woods? Of course I'd like to partake.

I asked him how much he charged and, to my total delight, the cost was about one seventh of what it cost in Penang. I did some mental calculations and it came out to twenty pipes for a dollar. That was dangerous, let me tell you. I remembered seeing a friend buying a gram of opium back home for 25 dollars and here it was ten grams for a dollar. Each prepared pipe was about a half gram.

This was opiate hog heaven and I later found out they had cemeteries just for travelers, where I'm sure 99 out of 100 who were buried there overdosed on heroin or morphine. The most powerful, pure opiates anywhere on earth and ridiculously cheap was a bad formula for the weak minded.

I lay my head on the head stool and, as the guy prepared the pipes, I was able to see into the kitchen where his wife was preparing a meal and kids were hanging onto her dress or playing on the floor nearby. This guy had a home business and I was soon one of his regular customers. I went there most days; morning, afternoon, and evening. I'd usually have ten pipes each visit. Blaine would almost always join me at least two times during the day if Zelda wasn't nagging him too much. She'd always say, "Blainnnnne," with a real nasal tone that bordered on annoying.

He enjoyed the whole scene and ritual of the smoking and just generally loved getting high but he did have a regular response to smoking the "big O" as we called it. It made him nauseous and he'd almost always puke as soon as we got up to leave the place where we smoked it.

In the mornings, after our morning "O," Blaine and I would stop by the house near Saylom Villa to purchase one of those cold yoghurts. We'd knock, a woman would open the door and walk over to her fridge and take out a couple of them for us. She made them with condensed milk so they were very sweet and tasty.

The next part of our routine was to go upstairs in the villa and hang out on one of the porches where there were chaises longues that we'd sit in while we slowly consumed the yoghurt. With that opium nod going, we'd sit there hardly moving, occasionally opening our eyes, realize we were holding a container of yoghurt, and then spoon some into our mouths and utter some kind of grunt that indicated the feeling of pleasure, and then inevitably drift back into our dreams and repeat.

It would take us a good hour to finish the yoghurt and maybe have a word with each other, conversations that went as far as, "Wow, this is nice," or Blaine's real trademark comment, "This is plez." Like clockwork, Zelda would come up and shake us a little and we'd then find ourselves in a trishaw heading over to the market for some chapati or to a café where people sat out and watched the world go by.

As the day progressed, and with a good meal inside us, we had a couple of options. One was to go sightseeing; there weren't that many great things to see in Vientiane. Two was my favorite option. There was a barber shop where I would go most days and, for about five cents, they'd give me a scalp massage for 30 minutes. That was nirvana for me.

I've loved scalp massages since I was a little kid when I'd lie on the couch with my head on my mom's lap and, while she was watching whatever program was on the TV, she'd continually stroke my head. My love for having my hair and head played with began right then and there. I enjoyed it very much and it was so evident that one of my cousins, Marjorie, would comb my hair for hours at a time when her family came over to visit.

There was one attraction in Vientiane, sort of an underground attraction, that I went to check out. Just outside the center of town was a large field with an old broken-down Chevy sitting in the middle of it. This was where the legendary Max the Roller did his work. You had to walk quite a way to the car. The passenger-side door was missing and inside the car there was no floor board. There was a large opening in the ground and you would step into the car and immediately go down a ladder to a room about eight feet below. A cave room. There was Max.

His business was taking a carton of cigarettes, opening it ever so gently so as to not mess up the cellophane the box was wrapped in, then he'd open each pack of cigarettes and empty out all the tobacco and then refill all two hundred cigarettes with the best marijuana you could provide him with. He was able to close each pack and attach the cellophane to the carton so nobody, especially a customs agent, would think to check a brand-new carton of cigarettes. He had a thriving business.

One of my favorite discoveries was the Café de la Paix. This was a French restaurant that had to be the finest place to eat in Vientiane. They had a five-course meal which included pâté with great French bread, French onion soup, coq au vin, filet mignon, or one of many other choices for the main course, a cheese plate, and then a crème brûlée or sorbet to finish it off. The house red wine also came with it and the cost was seventy-five cents. This wonderful place would be a problem for me in the weeks to come, as would any place at which I ate.

I'm walking around Vientiane with my joint ablaze.

VIENTIANE TO BANGKOK

I had the good fortune to meet and have fun with a couple of ladies from California. One of them was a lady I'd met in Jogja four months earlier; Santa Barbara Barbara is what we called her. She was a very attractive bleached blonde who rarely gave me the time of day in Jogja. There were plenty of guys down there she gravitated to and I didn't really pay much attention to her.

One day in Vientiane, while riding in a trishaw, it had slowed down at an intersection in an area with a few sidewalk cafés. Out of nowhere, here came Santa Barbara Barbara who jumped into the trishaw and hooked her arm under mine and said, "Hi, remember me?" I don't know if she was running from someone but I guess I was her choice for a friend to be with. Probably a bad choice for her, in retrospect.

We hung together for most of the day except for my afternoon opium smoking time. I think she thought it was fun the first few times when we'd go back to the villa, lie down together and cuddle and she'd lie there watching me while I was in dream city. After about four days, she got antsy. I was having dreams about everything under the sun and she was probably just dreaming that I'd get naked with her and get it on. She really gave it the All American Try but to no avail. I was not in any way rising to the occasion. She took off on the fifth day.

Shortly after that, I met Betty, a tall beautiful Chinese girl from Berkeley. She told me she'd applied for a visa to go to Cambodia and help those badly affected homeless and wounded in Battambang, the closest entry point into the country. She was totally fine with my impotence and would hang out with me all day, every day and even get naked and cuddle with me and we'd dream together. I really liked her and her dedication to go do something good for people where help was badly needed. I was pretty much just helping myself to massive quantities of cheap drugs. After one week, she got the visa and took off. Were those girls even real, I wondered? Blaine confirmed to me that they really were.

One of the best events in the villa was the day we celebrated Blaine's birthday. The upstairs room was a very large dormitory-like room where we went each morning after our smoke and purchase of the yoghurt. There were ten beds in this room along with a table and a few chairs. This is where we would celebrate Blaine's birthday with an afternoon bash. OK, maybe "bash" is misleading. Earlier in the day, we were walking back from our morning "O" session when we ran into a guy who wouldn't stop talking. He was funny though so we listened to his spiel.

He told us he was an AWOL soldier from the Vietnam War and had been on the run for at least two years. He'd just come from Luang Prabang and was getting the lie of the land in Vientiane. We asked him if he'd like to join us at the birthday party at our villa and he said he'd be there for sure.

At the party, there were a couple of Aussies who were traveling with a monkey. He was on a pretty lengthy rope. There was also a guy from New York City who sounded like Woody Allen. Another American guy, who didn't really participate in the celebrating, was there all day getting a tattoo on his back. The tattoo artist had a stick with three needles on the end and he'd keep dipping it in the ink and stabbing him over and over again, moving very slowly with his work. It was nothing like those tattoo guns that just buzz away and make it easy. Well, easier. There's a big difference between someone who knows how to use one and those who are not so good. The basic outline was there and it was the full length of his back, on one side. It was an old Asian man with a beard and he was holding a long staff.

So, this motley group were all sitting around telling travel stories and Zelda had gone out to find some snacks and a cake, although we had no idea where she was. The deserter showed up and promptly pulled out a mirror and opened a little packet which contained some China White heroin. He cut up very small lines, more like match-head size dots. He passed the mirror around and we all took turns snorting our share. Nobody was over zealous in taking more than they should.

After about an hour, the deserter was the only one talking. He had unlimited energy yet the rest of us were nodding with our heads bobbing up and down while scratching our noses. Enter Zelda. She came in the door with the cake in her hand and 30 candles lit, belting out, "Happy Birthday." Now the rest of us started in with the song but our volume and enthusiasm were very lacking compared to Zelda's and it was really a comedy watching a bunch of guys on the nod trying to sing in unison. We were pathetic.

I think the monkey was more in sync with Zelda and the deserter than the rest of us, by a long shot. It didn't matter. We all crowded around the table and Zelda cut up the cake. After the cake, we all sat back down on the beds and drifted off into nod-land.

*****

I was now getting very low on money and had just enough to get back to Bangkok and have three or four more days there before flying home. On my last day in Vientiane, I knew I had to conserve my money so, instead of paying for more pipes of opium, I went to the guy's house where I smoked and held up a large amount of marijuana. Probably an ounce and a half. I asked him, "How many pipes could I get for this?"

He told me, "None." He said marijuana was worth nothing. That really blew my mind. Not even one pipe would he part with. And me, such a great customer for several weeks.

Once again, I bid Blaine and Zelda goodbye and this time took the ferry back to Nong Khai and the bus down to Bangkok. I felt like some company and remembered that Andy, the Canadian Peace Corps friend, gave me Linda's phone number. I called her up and she said to come over to her house, giving me directions on how to get there. I headed over mid-afternoon. Now, I'd been in Laos, smoking a great deal of opium for several weeks and eating great food every day. Opium has a very constipating effect.

That whole time in Vientiane, I never once was able to have a bowel movement. It bothered me somewhat but I was so high on opium all the time I didn't really feel the same discomfort that you might if not under the influence of a major painkiller. So, there I was visiting with Linda and her roommate. We were having some tea and enjoying rehashing some of our experiences in Bali, where'd we met.

After not having had any opium now for a little more than two full days, I felt some activity in my stomach for the first time in ages. I think the caffeine in the tea was the catalyst. We had some more laughs and, after another twenty minutes, I really felt that something was about to happen. Linda pointed up the flight of stairs and said, "Turn left at the top and the bathroom is down the hall on the right."

When I sat down on the toilet, I was having major abdominal pains. Not much was happening though and I was rocking back and forth, trying to encourage something to occur. More pain and then nothing. I wondered if maybe this was what a woman feels like having contractions when giving birth. The pain was becoming more constant and I was sweating profusely, not just from the pain but also the heavy heat and humidity of midday in Bangkok. There was no air conditioning in that house.

I think about twenty minutes had gone by and I tried to care about what the girls would be thinking downstairs but I was really consumed by my condition. Now I felt a major pain and I grabbed onto a bar on the wall next to the toilet. That really did the trick. I pushed and pushed and slowly I felt something coming out of me. I was hysterical with glee, knowing for the

237

first time in almost a month something was happening other than a surgeon's knife potentially going in to remove the blockage, something I'd wondered might be the only way, many times while nodding on the "O."

I continued to hold onto that bar and push more and more. Finally, I felt "it" come free. I stood up and peered into the toilet and it looked like I passed a whole Presto log. It was standing on its end and, when I flushed the toilet, pretty much nothing happened other than the log turning on its end and rotating a little with the action of the water. In fact, the water started rising. It rose right up, until it started spilling out over the sides of the toilet and it was pouring down onto the tile floor.

I looked in horror as I tried to stop the water by jiggling the handle on the toilet but, just as that never worked at home, it wasn't working there either. I looked at the door and realized the bathroom floor was a sunken one. The floor of the bathroom was about three inches below the level of the bottom of the door and the hallway floor so I had a little time. But not enough. Now the water was filling up the whole bathroom and I freaked out when it went under the door into the hallway.

I was in major panic mode. A million thoughts went through my head about how I would explain this to Linda. I opened the door, sloshing with my flip-flops out into the hallway. I looked further along and saw a light coming from somewhere. I went over to what turned out to be a door and I opened it and saw a staircase leading down to an alley behind the house. I scampered down those stairs and ran three blocks until I knew I was safe. I don't have to tell you I never saw those girls again. I almost flew down the street, feeling so light on my feet.

*****

At my hotel, I met a guy and we traded travel stories. He told me he was always on the lookout for good semi-precious stones. I had a few rubies I'd picked up along the way and he bought them for a couple of hundred dollars. All of a sudden, I wasn't in a bad position. I was able to make a reservation to fly with China Airlines to San Francisco via Saigon, then on to Hawaii and then home. I reached the airport with plenty of time to spare. When I checked in, the agent at the desk asked me if I'd like to stop in Saigon. Hmmm, I'd never given Saigon any consideration but, yes, I decided I'd really like to see the place.

I was told I could stay as long as I wanted with no extra charge and continue on my journey by just calling them the day before I wanted to continue on to Hawaii. I figured I could stay almost a week if I didn't blow my money foolishly. I went to the lounge and actually fell asleep. Some time later, someone shook me awake. It was a lady from China Airlines, asking me if I was supposed to be on the flight to Saigon. I said yes, so she called someone downstairs. They came to get me and I was taken down below where we got on a set of motorized passenger stairs that drove me out to the plane that had already departed the terminal. It was waiting just for me. The door opened and I walked in, greeted by many dirty looks from fellow passengers as I took my seat. *Vietnam, here I come.*

FROM VIETNAM TO MILL VALLEY

After landing at Saigon's airport, I took a taxi into the city. The road from the airport was littered on both sides by abandoned U.S. military vehicles — armored personnel carriers, jeeps, Deuce and a Halfs, and more. It seemed as if there were hundreds of them on either side of the road.

I found a nice hotel that was still fairly cheap. On the streets was an endless line of young people riding bicycles. The thing that really jumped out at me was that all the girls rode along wearing their long, flowing *áo dài* over black pajama-style pants. It was a beautiful thing to see. It was late so I just ate at the hotel restaurant and turned in.

The next day was excellent as I walked down a really wide beautiful street that looked like it was a popular hangout. I had a bowl of noodles and a couple of beers and was just loving the place. There were no US soldiers anywhere.

After I left the restaurant I'd been lounging in, I was greeted by two very lovely Vietnamese ladies. One spoke very good English and asked, "Are you an American?"

"Why yes, I am," I responded, somewhat taken aback by her boldness.

"Are you in the military?" she continued.

"No, I'm just a civilian traveling around South-East Asia."

"Oh, well, we really miss the American soldiers who we had a lot of fun with and made lots of money from," she said. "Would you like to party with my friend and me?"

"Believe me," I said, "I would love to party with the two of you but I'm on my way home and I'm pretty much broke, with just enough to pay for my hotel and a little food."

She floored me. "What if I said this one is on my friend and me and you needn't pay us at all?"

That was an easy one to answer. "My hotel's right around the corner. Let's go."

We headed to my room and the two of them stripped down and put on a wonderful show for me. Then they waved me over to join in with them. That just might be the best gift ever.

241

The next afternoon, I was really in the mood for smoking some opium. I figured this would be a piece of cake to get together. I went outside my hotel and waved a trishaw over to the curb and told him I would like to go somewhere I'd be able to smoke some opium. He shrugged his shoulders, not understanding a word I'd said. So, I used my hands to demonstrate and acted out like I was holding the bamboo pipe and putting it into my mouth and inhaling. He smiled and gestured for me to get into the back.

He rode and he rode for at least twenty blocks, weaving through cars and bicycles. He finally pulled up to a monument and stopped. He got off the trishaw and walked over to two seductively dressed women. He spoke with them and the three of them came back over to me. One of the women said to me, "You want a blow job?" I broke out laughing. The trishaw driver misunderstood my demonstration of smoking a pipe for something he had probably heard from western tourists on a more regular basis. I told her that wasn't what I wanted and mentioned smoking a pipe. She nodded and spoke to the driver about what I *really* wanted.

I got back in and he peddled the twenty blocks back to my hotel and pointed to another trishaw driver and told him what I wanted. The new trishaw took me in another direction altogether. It was getting dark now and we were in an area of town that looked like a place that no tourist ever went, day or night. It concerned me a little but I knew the houses and areas I smoked opium in other parts of Asia were also off the beaten track.

The driver stopped at a house and went up the staircase and knocked on the door. An old guy with a scraggly long white beard and wearing black pajamas spoke with him. I told the driver I only wanted to spend five dollars and no more and that he should tell the old man. He walked me into the house and up a ladder to the next floor. It was a small room with a few candles lighting it to a dingy glow at best. The old man took my five dollars-worth of Vietnamese dong and gave it to the driver, telling him where he could go to find what I wanted. I was excited as hell and figured I'd got twenty pipes to a dollar in Laos so, even though this was the city, I should get a very good amount to smoke for five dollars.

While the driver was gone, the old man lit up a half-smoked joint that was sitting in the ash tray and we passed it back and forth and smiled a lot. He kept gesturing the driver would be back soon with what I was looking for. After 30 minutes or so, the driver came back and handed the old man a packet. I became giddy like a kid the night before Christmas.

The old guy started preparing my first pipe. It wasn't the traditional bamboo one I was smoking in Penang and Vientiane but I didn't put much emphasis on the type of pipe. It was the opium I was interested in anyway. He finished the first one, handed me the end, and held the flame up to the bowl. I inhaled that wonderful smoke, feeling like I'd reconnected with an old friend.

He prepared another pipe and again I smoked it and was feeling like I was on my way. After the third pipe, he got up and I wondered why, in the middle of smoking some opium, he would do that. I figured we were just getting started. To my dismay, he was getting up because that five dollars only bought enough "O" for three pipes. I started to get a little testy but then remembered I was in the middle of a ghetto, in a strange place, and I had no idea where I'd go if I ran out the door. Or what might happen to me in that neighborhood at night.

So, I thanked the old guy, tipped him, and the driver took me back to my hotel. I was frustrated over that whole experience. Back at my hotel, I called room service and ordered a meal. While I was at it, I asked the concierge if he had a girl he could send to my room. He said he'd check into it and called me back fifteen minutes later. He had someone who could come to my room for only one hour as she was with another guest in the hotel for the whole night but the guest didn't mind her leaving for an hour. That was fine with me.

There was a knock on the door and I opened it and there was a beautiful lady who said, "Hi," gave the thumbs-up sign and said, "Oh, you're number one." I guessed she liked me. After an hour, just like the concierge said, she looked at the clock on my night stand, gave me a hug and a smile, and off she went.

RETURNING HOME

I decided to leave the next day, called the airline, and booked a flight to Honolulu. I have an uncle who'd been living in Honolulu since the early '60s after getting his PhD in anthropology from Stanford. He was a professor and the head of the anthropology department at the University of Hawaii. I decided to go visit him and possibly stay in Oahu for a while before continuing home. I didn't know how to reach him by phone so, when I got off the plane, I took a taxi to the University. I asked where I could find my uncle and they showed me a map of the campus and I walked over to his office. It was my lucky day. He was there and we had a big hug and he closed up for the day and took me back to his condo.

All the way there, he told me how he would love for me to stay with him and his wife for as long as I wanted and just enjoy Oahu. He even said I could use his car during the day as long as I'd be back at the campus in time to pick him up when he got off work. When I first saw him at his office and he hugged me he commented, "Boy you really smell, Kenny." I reminded him I'd left my hotel in Saigon on a hot humid day more than a dozen hours ago and had been flying all day and then, after arriving in Oahu, I was subjected to more hot and humid weather and walking all over the campus in that heat and carrying my two daypacks.

We pulled into the garage of his condo complex and went up to his home. His wife was there to greet me and, with no restraint at all, she told me to immediately get into the shower so we could all enjoy inhabiting the same room. When I came out, we had a great time talking about my travels and what had been going on with family around the USA while I'd been gone. I think I was still a little spaced out from all the drugs I'd been doing and raised their eyebrows with a couple of my stories. We had dinner and my aunt washed, dried, and folded all my dirty clothes. When I went to bed, I was still under the impression I'd be staying with them for at least a week or two.

The next morning, my uncle woke me up, shaking me in my bed. He whispered, "Ken, if you get your things together quickly, I can drop you off at the airport in time for you to catch the 10 a.m. flight to San Francisco." Was this real? What an about-face from the day before. Sure enough, after rubbing my eyes a lot, he was still standing there, urging me to get out of bed. *Well, OK, you gotta roll with it,* is what I always thought. After a quick and unemotional goodbye, my uncle took off for his day at the office, probably breathing many sighs of relief. I headed for the departure gate.

All those months earlier, when Debbie and I had been on our way to Asia together initially, flying on China Airlines, we noticed something strange on that flight. Namely the passengers, who all looked like they were suffering from one thing or another. I'd found the leader of the group and asked why they seemed different. She told me they were all going to Manila to see if a world-famous faith healer could help them. They'd all tried for years to cure their problems with conventional medicine and this was their last-ditch effort to get well again. She told me she'd been with a group the year before and, although she wasn't suffering from any illness, she let the faith healer examine her. He reached into her and pulled out some bloody tissue and said he had removed a cancerous tumor. He told her that, if she'd gone another year or two, her cancer would have spread to a point where even chemo would not have helped her to survive. She was hooked and even tried to get Debbie and me to join them the following day for a flight from Taiwan to Manila. We declined.

So, there I was, sitting in one of the chairs in the waiting area, ready to fly back to San Francisco, and who should I see but that very woman! I asked her how that trip went. She told me it didn't go well. Several of the people stayed in the hotel in Taiwan, refusing to continue on. The faith healer turned out to be a scam artist and her company was being sued in a class action suit. She stayed in Oahu after returning from Asia and was finally going back to the mainland to get her life together. Small world moment.

I returned to San Francisco and immediately called Debbie's sister's house to see if Debbie was back yet. Linda answered the phone and told me to come over so she could hear all the stories I had to tell. She said Debbie wasn't there and she'd tell me all about it when I got there. Once there, she told me how Debbie spent the next couple of months in Batu Ferringhi, drinking at the bar of a really nice resort hotel not far from where our little metal shack was.

"When I went to pick up Debbie up at the airport," Linda told me, "she came to the waiting area and you could smell the booze on her. She was so blasted from all the drinking on the flight, I knew she needed help right away so I took her straight to Mount Zion Hospital and checked her into the detox ward, where she'd also spent a good amount of time before I introduced you to her. Once she was admitted, the detox ward administrator gave me all of Debbie's belongings. When I got back to Mill Valley, I emptied Debbie's purse out on the kitchen table and found about 40 balls of opium."

I was pretty shocked she made it through customs without getting caught with them. "Linda, those were the leftover balls of opium I purchased when we were in Penang, while we were waiting for the cowboy shirts to be made." I was all of a sudden pretty excited. Forty balls of opium made it back to Mill Valley! "So, where are those balls of opium if you don't mind my asking?"

"Ken, you've got to be kidding. You think they're still around? Hahaha! I had a few friends over the next week, every night, and we smoked it all up. Thank you for your opium but it's all gone, baby."

Bastards. Those were mine. Debbie really never liked the opium as much as a few stiff drinks. I told Linda, "Debbie and I went shopping in Singapore for the fabric for the cowboy shirts and then, after her having sex with two guys in our bungalow while I was sick as a dog, I told her I was leaving and she said she'd send me money to pay her share at my next destination, Jogjakarta, but she never did."

"Look, Ken, Debbie's visiting family down in Palm Springs right now so, if you want to wait until she gets back to get your money, that's about the only option. But to be honest, she's pretty broke so I don't know if you'll get your money when she gets back. If you want, you can go in her closet and take some of her designer clothes to make up for what you think is fair to repay you."

"Well, if you're OK with that, then that's what I'm going to do."

I went up to Debbie's room and opened the closet. She had five or six really nice dresses from Paris in there. She was the same size as two of my friends' wives were. I took all of them and later gave them away to the ladies.

*****

I had one other loose end to tie up. There was a notice from U.S. Customs that some packages were waiting for me to pick up at a cargo storage building at San Francisco Airport. I was very excited. The shirts had arrived and I was about to take the first step toward starting a business that could take me, on a regular basis, to the part of the world I had just fallen in love with. With the revenue from the shirts, I could go back and order a larger number of shirts to build my momentum. I knew friends would see how well I did the first time around and want to invest and make some money of their own. It brings to mind a saying, "Man plans, God laughs."

I got to the airport cargo area and filled out lots of paperwork and then put the boxes of shirts into my car. When I got back to my mom and dad's house, I quickly opened one of the boxes. Each shirt was packaged very professionally in clear plastic and, as I opened one and pulled out the shirt, it had the cardboard in the collar and everything, just like if you bought a shirt at Macy's. When I unfolded the shirt, it seemed like a whole lot of fabric. The workmanship looked first rate but something was wrong.

I looked for a medium and put it on. Now my heart was racing. The sleeves were two inches above my wrists. What was worse, if anything can top sleeves being way too short, the body of the shirt was straight down instead of angling inwards to be form fitting. Form-fitted shirts were the rage at that time and these shirts were not form fitting. They looked silly.

I opened a couple more to see if they were all the same and even the large and extra-large had sleeve lengths that were for tiny guys. I had to calm myself down. *Just go sell the shirts in the packaging and you'll be fine*, I told myself. *I mean, without a doubt they look great wrapped up.* I went to a few stores around Marin County and finally parked in Sausalito with my brother, Rick, and walked into the nicest men's clothing store around, Gene Hillers. I wanted to sell the shirts for $25 each, knowing a store like that could easily double the price.

I took in five different shirts with various combinations of fabric. The manager of the store flipped and said, "Yes, we'll buy all you have. All one hundred." I was ready to do the transaction right there but he then stopped my excitement, albeit temporarily, telling me he had to wait until the owner showed up in two hours. He said I was to call him back and he'd have the official OK by then. After that, I could bring him all the shirts and he'd have a check for me for $2,500. I was ecstatic.

Rick and I went to a great restaurant on the water, got the best table overlooking Belvedere Island, and we toasted each other. He had a cherry coke and I had a beer. Life couldn't get any better. After lunch, we walked around town, killing the two hours until I would have my windfall. It was time.

I walked into Gene Hillers and saw the manager. He had a strange look on his face. Then came the crushing blow. He told me he and the owner opened up a couple of the packages and they thought I was playing a bad joke on them. Was I for real? These shirts were garbage. He handed them back to me and told me to never come into the store and try and pull a fast one on them again. That really hurt.

I knew I blew it by not staying in Singapore and having the tailors do a trial run then staying until they got it right. Ken's folly. I gave the shirts away to friends who mostly used them to wash their cars. A few just cut off the sleeves and, with a cowboy hat, had a good Halloween costume. Marin rednecks.

On the way home, out of nowhere and so unlikely but very fitting, the song "I'm a Loser" by the Beatles came on. Rick and I just broke up laughing. What more can I say…

CONTACT THE AUTHOR

I sincerely thank you for reading this book and hope you enjoyed it. I would be extremely grateful if you could leave a review on Amazon.

I'd love to hear your comments and am happy to answer any questions you may have. Do please get in touch with me by:

Email: moeliss@me.com

Facebook: www.facebook.com/moeliss

I look forward to hearing from you.

Kenneth Liss

ACKNOWLEDGMENTS

I would like to thank:

My first wife for leaving me for a friend of mine which became the catalyst for getting my interest in travel up and running. Since that time, I've never stopped dreaming about travel if I wasn't already traveling.

My good friend and mentor/editor/publisher, Jacky Donovan, for her friendship, great work, and constant encouragement.

Friends and family who used to respond to my telling travel stories with, "You should write a book."

Kamala Thomas, owner of Webcraft Asia, for taking my low-resolution photos and making them look so much better.

My wife of 42 years, Dara, for her role in inspiring me to sit still for hours at a time and write it all down. May she be luxuriating in heaven for all eternity.

My lucky stars for helping me find Tran Thi Hue, my adorable and most wonderful loving wife, to spend the rest of my life with.

ABOUT THE AUTHOR

Born in San Francisco, Ken Liss graduated from high school in 1966 and went to College of San Mateo then University of California, Berkeley where he spent his time mixing academics, LSD, and watching anti-Vietnam War demonstrations on the campus and adjoining Telegraph Avenue. He attended many live music shows in the early days of Fillmore Auditorium, Winterland, and free shows in Golden Gate Park, developing eclectic musical tastes.

After two years in the Army National Guard, he was released four years early after claiming to an army psychiatrist he had dreams of punishing his superior officers. Following a short marriage, which ended abruptly in 1972, he began traveling in Europe where he caught the travel bug. Today, he lives with his Vietnamese wife and her two daughters in Sihanoukville, Cambodia, and enjoys day after day relaxing and meeting travelers on the beaches of the Gulf of Thailand.

Made in United States
Orlando, FL
11 January 2022

13281235R00157